# Dried Flowers for Decoration

Helichrysum, foliage and grasses (*Leslie Johns*)

# Dried Flowers for Decoration

Violet Stevenson

DAVID & CHARLES
NEWTON ABBOT

*ISBN 0 7153 5517 1*

First published in 1955 by W. H. & L. Collingridge Ltd
Second revised edition published by David & Charles in 1972
New impression 1973

Printed in Great Britain
by Redwood Press Limited Trowbridge Wiltshire
for David & Charles (Holdings) Limited
South Devon House Newton Abbot Devon

# Contents

# Illustrations

*All the photographs are from the author's collection*

# *Introduction*

'Dried flowers' do not mean the same to all people. If you have never experimented with more than a winter vase of statice and helichrysum or have been content with a jug of teasels and rushes, then an exciting new world awaits you! If perhaps you haven't thought much about the subject at all, except to wish that you could find some floral decoration that would withstand the heat and the drying atmosphere of a centrally heated interior and still last for months or even years, then I can offer a solution to your problem.

Since I first wrote in praise of dried flower arrangements I have watched them gradually come to play an increasingly important role in interior decoration, and I like to think that I have been responsible for ousting artificial and plastic flowers from many places. Who really wants these when the world is full of real plant materials ready waiting, often only for the searching, for the best are usually free! And what a variety they offer, both in themselves and also in the many ways in which they can be displayed. In my own home they not only often decorate the table centre, brighten and fill a corner, stand displayed on a shelf or fill an empty fireplace, but they also frame a mirror, furnish a wall and accentuate an archway.

From this you can tell that the materials I use must vary considerably if they are to play so many roles. The term 'dried flowers' is an umbrella. Under it you will find not only the true 'immortelles' and 'everlastings' but also some familiar fresh flowers that will retain some of their characteristics after drying, such as delphiniums and alchemilla; the seed vessels of other flowers which resemble wooden or leathery blooms such as fritillaria and poppy; the cases of

8

nuts and fruits and pine cones, some from trees and shrubs all around us and others from countries overseas; grasses, rushes and all kinds of leaves along with fungi, lichens, branches, spathes, roots and all parts of plants so long as they have some claim to beauty.

Since I believe that flower arrangement is important only because it leads the enthusiast along many avenues to a wider and happier life, I have always been intensely interested in the collection and the arrangement of these dried or semi-permanent plant materials. I am unashamedly in love with all things that grow. It is difficult for me to understand why some people should think that a bare seed is not as lovely in its own way as the flowers locked deep in its closely guarded cells. And it does not surprise me to learn that the flower arrangers who begin taking a keen interest in this pleasant art because they love fresh flowers, end up by becoming absorbed in the collection and display of those parts left on a plant after its flowers have gone.

On the whole, dried flowers—or perpetuelles as I like to call them—can be treated and displayed in exactly the same manner as fresh materials and their sparse lines and subdued hues exploited to the full, or the two kinds, fresh and dried, can be mixed, one providing the delicacy to complement the robustness of the other. On the other hand, because they don't have to be stood in water, they can be used in many designs unsuitable for fresh flowers.

The designs into which you set these materials will depend on you; I can only guide. To do this, I have written chapters on the assembly and arrangement of perpetuelles as well as on drying and on what type of materials to grow and collect. I hope that after you have read this book you will be inspired to experiment, to grow, gather, harvest and glean and to share your enjoyment with others as I have tried to do here.

# CHAPTER 1

# Drying

Some flowers and plant materials can be arranged as soon as they are gathered and they will slowly dry in situ. If this should not be convenient and it would be better to store them, then it is absolutely essential that they are thoroughly dried. If any moisture remains in any part they will become mouldy during storage. The method of drying for these is quite simply to hang them in an airy place. Others have to be treated differently.

There are three main methods I use and to a large extent the use of one method or the other depends upon the type of flower. To simplify matters as much as possible, I have classified the methods under three headings.

## Method 1, by natural means

This is the most ancient and is both simple and effective so long as certain points are observed. The most important factor is that the materials should be quite dry when they are gathered and that this dryness is maintained in the surroundings in which they are hung.

Where foliage on the stem of a flower or, in the case of

10

subjects such as physalis, the seed case, is soft and lush, it should be stripped. Thick downy leaves as occur on some helichrysums and allied flowers and achillea for instance, can be safely left on the stem. Later they may contribute to the arrangement.

The flowers and other plant materials should be made into small bunches, stem ends roughly level. Too many in a bunch prevent air circulating freely among the blooms. Heads set on a level do not become as aired as those at varying levels. Stems should be tied very tightly because they shrink as they dry. My own method is to use a long 22 gauge florists' wire, one end of which can quickly be bound round the stems while the other end can be hooked and hung over a rail or line. When the stems shrink it is a simple matter to pull the wire a little tighter. Unless bunches are inspected from time to time the contents are likely to fall out.

Canes stretched from one point to another or retractable clothes' lines which can be closed when not in use, are needed to hang the bunches. These should be hung at different levels, again to facilitate the movement of air. The bunches should be hung head downwards and the stems arranged and tied so that they are as straight as possible. Although a curved stem is often an advantage when arranging flowers, dried stems are apt to become broken at the point where they bend or curve.

The place in which the bunches are hung should be cool, airy and shady. Never dry perpetuelles under glass because the bright light draws out their colours and also makes them brittle. The shadier the conditions in which you dry grass, for example, the more lifelike its colour will be.

In most cases it is helpful if flowers retain their stems. Some hang on tenaciously but others are so brittle that the heads become easily severed. Yet others, *Helichrysum bracteatum* in particular, also have unattractive stems when

11

dried. These flowers and any with similar characteristics are best beheaded when they are gathered and laid out to dry, either on newspaper on a bench or, and more to be recommended, in a hammock or on a shelf made of netting so that the air can pass round all parts of the blooms. The flowers themselves dry well but there is a disadvantage in that they are difficult to mount on false stems. Ways and means to do this are given in Chapter 10 but I think that this is the place to describe a method I now most frequently use.

Cut the flower with about an inch of stem and, while this is still succulent and the bloom soft, take a 20 gauge wire (use finer wires for smaller subjects) and insert it up the flower's centre. Do not let the wire pierce the centre so that it becomes visible from the top. As the flowers dries the wire stem will rust and hold in place. Wires are really quite inconspicuous. Later they can be easily hidden by other components of the arrangements.

Start off with long wires. It is much easier to shorten these than to elongate them. To dry flowers mounted this way, I use weighted containers topped with blocks of Oasis, a lightweight foamed plastic substance much used for flower arrangement and available all over the world. Its convenience lies in the fact that a stem inserted into it will be held, gently but securely, in the required position at once. It may be used dry but will absorb water readily, so suits both fresh and dried flowers. Used as described here, the wires are inserted in Oasis, each flower being well spaced.

Flowers suitable for drying this way include *Achillea filipendula*, ammobium, anaphalis, catananche, gomphrena, helichrysum, helipterum, limonium or statice, both annual and perennial; lonas and xeranthemum. All green seed heads, cereals and other grasses, flowering stems of grey-leaved shrubs in bud such as senecio and grey and evergreen foliage can also be dried this way.

One point on harvesting, try to cut flowers so that any side shoots present are left to develop into more flowers. In many cases, this may mean that stems are fairly short but this is not of great significance.

## Method 2, by dry heat in a dark place

The 'everlastings' and 'immortelles' are natural 'dried' flowers. Even if we did not hang them to dry slowly, their petals and bracts would still have their characteristic papery texture. The main reason we harvest them as we do is because we want to have the flowers at their best. Left on the plant they would become too mature and when they do this they become fluffy with seed and less bright in colour.

These flowers, mainly Australasian and South African, or native to other parts of the latter continent, are true driers yet there are many others without the natural characteristics of the former which also will dry. Their colours will never be as bright in death as they were in life, nor, in most cases, will their outlines be so clear cut. Often too, it seems that such flowers are dried by a lucky chance for one cannot always repeat a great success of a former year. Much depends upon the maturity of a flower, the state of the weather, not only when it was gathered but also of the preceding weeks, and perhaps most of all, the conditions under which the materials are dried. The best method I have discovered is by dry heat in a dark place.

When by accident I discovered that the best way to dry delphiniums is very quickly in an airing cupboard (and, incidentally, I was dealing with very large spikes produced at the end of the season), I experimented with many other flowers with varying results. Now I use the cupboard at all times of the year for a great and increasing variety.

The slatted shelves in the cupboard are ideal because individual flowers, such as hydrangeas, may be hung from them (use florists' wire twisted round the stem end and the other end hooked over the slat), while flat flowers, such as zinnias, can be supported by them, their stems pushed through the slats. The warm air thus circulates well round the thickest part of the bloom.

It is not possible to say how long the drying period should be because this depends on many factors; the condition of the flower, its size and the air volume inside the cupboard. Darkness is essential so do not attempt to use any other warm dry place unless light can be excluded.

## Method 3, by use of dessicants

The variety of everlastings and all the other flowers and plant materials which I group under the omnibus heading of perpetuelles is so great as to be sufficient for most decorative purposes. Even so, there are many people who would like to know how to dry sappy flowers such as orchids, dahlias, daffodils and gentians.

To dry these a dessicant must be used. The oldest and cheapest process is that by which flowers are buried in dry, clean sand. The greatest drawback to this method is that the sand is so heavy that it often damages the flowers. On the other hand the weight is no disadvantage when 'faced' flowers, pansies for example, are to be dried. Furthermore, since flowers of this type take up little space, only a shallow layer of sand is needed to cover them, so the risk of bruising is not so great. Generally speaking, the drying process using sand takes from three to four weeks.

Sand can be mixed with other dessicants, usually domestic borax and silicagel, a form of ground quartz combined with an absorbent chemical, in the proportion of one part sand, previously thoroughly dried in an oven, to two parts of powdered borax or silicagel crystals. I have been told that cornmeal can be substituted for either of these but I have not tried it myself. Silicagel alone can also be used. This is lighter in weight but more expensive. However, it can be used time and time again after being dried, as can the other dessicants.

The dessicant draws the water from the flowers' tissues. When they feel dry to the touch they may be removed and arranged. In dry atmospheres they will dry even further but if there is any marked degree of moisture in the atmosphere they are likely to absorb it and may need to be dessicated once more.

The flowers are dried in boxes. Tall spikes, if it is required to dry these whole, can be stood in tall cylinders. Arrange these so that they can be opened either end and remove the flowers stem-ends first. Either bury the flowers by pouring the dessicant over them as they lie on a bottom layer of it, or, in the case of cupped and deep flowers, support them on a grid of wire-netting fitted into the box. Pour the dessicant in carefully, taking care that it runs into the interstices of the petals and that, finally, it smothers them.

Inspecting the flowers is often a little tricky because one must take care not to damage the buried flowers as one searches for them. One way of uncovering them is to pour off the sand from below. Make holes in the floor of the box before it is filled, and cover these with adhesive tape. Uncover one or more holes so that the sand runs out. As the flowers are revealed the holes can be temporarily re-covered. If the petals are not dry enough it is a simple matter to pour the sand back over them again from the top.

The range both of the kinds and colours of flowers which can be dried by this process is very wide. The most difficult subjects are those which are thick and fleshy. For instance,

## DRYING

I found that cymbidiums browned yet gladioli became so papery that they easily disintegrated. I was able to use the brown orchid in an arrangement and I found that the gladioli, which was not suitable for use, needed only a brief time in the dessicant, which is really a little surprising when one considers the texture of the flowers.

Multi-petalled and/or fleshy flowers such as dahlias, zinnias, double daisies of all kinds, and some others should be buried until the broad outer petals are dry, and then finished off in a warm cupboard to ensure that every drop of moisture has evaporated.

The drying period necessary for certain flowers can only be gauged by experiment but it is seldom a long one. In some cases, hours not days are involved. Small roses, frail annuals, nigella for instance and pansies, may be ready in twelve hours. The first time I dried cornflowers, *Centaurea cyanus*, I gave them three days, thirty-six hours would have been sufficient. By the time I inspected them the flowers had become so dry that they shattered. This was not only due to the length of time they had remained buried. Shattering is a tendency with some flowers, even when they are dessicated only for a short period. To avoid this happening, fix the petals by painting the bases with a touch of gum arabic. This is time-consuming, so it must remain a personal decision as to whether or not it is worth while. In some cases the calyx has to be glued to the petals otherwise the bloom disintegrates. This fault is most prevalent among the compositae and single daisies in particular. Flat, disc like daisies should be buried face downwards.

Labiate or lipped flowers such as snapdragons (antirrhinums) and foxgloves (digitalis) need to have the base of the lip anchored to the calyx before drying. As a general rule, all those which tend to drop in fresh arrangements and not merely fade on the stems, should be wired by making a tiny

*Page 17* True everlastings in white helichrysum, anaphalis, gnaphalium, rhodanthe, ammobium and limonium in variety with
honesty, briza and meadow grasses (p24)

*Page 18* Wheat, oats, barley and maize with skeletonised lime (tilia) and pressed field maple leaves, poppy seed heads and white limonium in wicker covered wine-bottle

hairpin of very fine wire and pushing it from one side of the calyx, pinning the end of the corolla inside it, to the other side.

Large spicate flowers such as gladioli, delphiniums and hollyhocks are best first divided, the individual 'pips' or florets mounted on false stems of wire and dried as individuals. Later, they may be re-assembled (Chapter 10) or used as individually mounted separate blooms.

Subsequent mounting and assembly is often made much simpler if the flower is wired while fresh. A short length of wire, its gauge dependent on the size and frailty of the flower, can either be inserted up into the centre of the stem or laid parallel to it.

Hollow stems are easily wired internally but solid fleshy stems may be much more difficult to penetrate. For flowers that are not wired internally, it is usual to pass the tip of the wire into the base of the flower and then to pass the rest of the wire round the stem. However, inserting the tip of the wire into the flower may cause it to disintegrate later when it has become dried and for this reason it may be best simply to lay the wire against the short stem and tape the two together using florists' tape or crepe 'stem' paper, the rolls cut across to make $\frac{1}{4}$in thick ribbons.

In most cases it is best to shorten stems and mount them on short wires using one or other of these methods before drying. Wires can be lengthened later in various ways which are described elsewhere.

## Storage

Many of the perpetuelles I use are several years old. Often they are taken out of store, displayed and returned to their boxes and bags. If while they have been on display they have become very dusty (something which inevitably happens if they are in London) or if they have been on show all winter, they are first washed in warm water and detergent, dried thoroughly, usually by laying them on newspaper in a warm room, before being returned to store.

Transparent plastic bags, each holding one type of material, are either fastened at the mouth with a wire and hung by crooking the other end, or they are placed in well-labelled boxes. Flower bunches are best hung with their stem ends at the bottom of the bag.

Ferns and leaves pressed between pages of magazines are best stored that way. They may also be stacked one leaf above the other with a tissue or piece of paper between each and placed in polythene bags or in boxes.

It is essential that all perpetuelles should be kept in a dry, fairly warm place, or they will become mouldy. If they can only be kept in an outer shed, sprinkle a little silicagel in the bag or box to absorb moisture and change it frequently if it changes colour. Make the bags and boxes as airtight as possible. Inspect the materials in store in such a place frequently.

## Skeleton leaves or shadow leaves

Certain shadow or skeleton leaves can be bought from the florists' sundriesman. Called magnolia, they are in fact, often ficus. The leaves are sold bleached and dyed in several hues and are very beautiful and extremely long lasting. Although often expensive they will last and remain decorative for many years if they are carefully washed, rinsed and dried when they become dingy.

When marketed these leaves are packed flat and are often too rigid to be really pleasing when arranged. Curves are easily induced. Beginning at the tip of the leaf, curl it round a pencil for an acute curve; round a thicker object, a candle for example, for a slight curve. To get the degree of curve required, pull the leaf out flat and allow it to spring back to the amount of curve needed. If it is still too tight repeat the operation until the leaf is just as wanted.

Tough-textured leaves can be skeletonised in rain water by natural methods. Crowd but entirely immerse the leaves in a vessel and stand it out of doors in the sun for several weeks. Top up the water level when required. It is essential that there is bacterial activity in the water which means it will become smelly and slimy! It should not be changed because the greater this activity, the quicker will the soft tissues of the leaves disintegrate. The fleshy upper and undersides will rot and the tough central portion will remain.

Inspect the leaves from time to time after the first four weeks. Rub a leaf gently between finger and thumb. Eventually it should become slippery and the outer tissues colourless. At this point it should be possible to pull the outer surfaces away. Insert a point, a darning needle is good for this, near the midrib at the stem end. If the leaf is ready you should be able easily to lift the layers and peel them away from the tissue skeleton. This should be done gently. The shadow leaf should then be washed under a tap until all the green tissue is gone—a matter of a few moments. If the leaves are discoloured they may be made cleaner by soaking them in water to which domestic bleach has been added. Dry them by laying them as flat as they will go on newspaper. They may then be stored.

Leaves which have fallen or have turned colour are better than green leaves because their skeletons are mature. Laurel, camellia, oak, maple, lime, holly, pear are just a few which can be treated this way. All are worth experimenting with.

Holly and some other evergreens fall in a thick mat below

their tree. Some of these leaves, usually faded in colour, can be quickly skeletonised in the following manner. Pour boiling water over the leaves in the bowl. Add a teaspoon of domestic bleach to a pint of water and leave to soak. Test after three days. Before bleaching, reject all leaves with brown tough blotches on the skin.

In an 1884 issue of *Amateur Gardening* I came across this recipe for skeletonising leaves. Some readers might like to try this quicker method.

Dissolve 3oz of washing soda in two pints of boiling water, and add 1½oz of slaked quick lime; boil for ten minutes, decant the clear solution and bring it to the boil. While boiling add the leaves; boil briskly for some time—say an hour, occasionally adding hot water to replace that lost by evaporation. Take out a leaf [with tongs!], put it into a vessel of water and rub it between the fingers under the water. If the skin separates easily, remove the rest of the leaves and treat them in the same way; if not, the boiling must be continued some time longer. To bleach the skeletons, mix about a drachm of chloride of lime with a pint of water, adding sufficient acetic acid to liberate the chlorine. Steep the leaves in this till they are whitened (about ten minutes), taking care not to let them stay in too long, or they may become brittle. Put them into clean water, and float them out on pieces of paper. Lastly, remove them from the paper before they are quite dry and press them.

Another method is as follows. Use this for tough leathery leaves only, such as ficus, magnolia, fatsia, thick maples, etc. Use an old pan or tin because this process will damage a good vessel. Make a strong solution of soda and rain water. Boil the leaves until they are pulpy. Lay them on a newspaper, one at a time—let the others remain soaking but not boiling—and gently scrape off the pulp from the skeleton with the back of a knife. Well rinse the leaves in clean water. Soak in household bleach and dry.

Some bracts or similar structures, eg hydrangeas, physalis, nicandra, may also be skeletonised in the same way as described for leaves. There is a right and wrong time to do this. Wait until the textures have changed and they are tough and leathery. This means allowing the materials to remain on the plant as long as possible at the end of the flowering season and even to have a touch of frost because this hastens disintegration. Readers who live away from frosts can place the materials, wrapped in plastic sheeting or in bags, in the deepfreeze for a day or two. My most successful skeletonised hydrangeas have been from those which had over-wintered on the plant and had turned quite brown.

Remove any of these from the stagnant water as soon as they are ready, wash well, bleach if required and dry by hanging them in a warm, dry place.

Sometimes, natural skeletons of leaves, bracts, seed heads and even other parts of plants can be found. Malope seed structures, for instance, very quickly become skeletons and remain firmly fixed on their stems producing something which is both beautiful and graceful. Often these natural shadow forms are damaged and soiled. But, having noted the facility of such materials easily to produce an attractive skeleton, the arranger can gather them earlier another year and prepare better samples by following any of the methods given. Any such materials should be gathered as soon as they turn colour and/or texture. These can always be lightened by bleaching or darkened by dyeing.

The stems of skeletons become affected by the processing and often consist of a collection of fibres which fray easily. These may be reinforced with wire when they are mounted.

# CHAPTER 2

# *True everlastings*

Since I first wrote about dried flowers and perpetuelles, many from all over the world have passed through my hands and in my travels I have seen others. Some were familiar, some not, although in most cases they were either recognisable or identifiable. All have engaged my interest and aroused my enthusiasm. Many of the flowers were species of helichrysum and allied plants of Africa; others were American and Australasian. (See plate p17.)

One assumes that, because of the present and ever-growing interest in perpetuelle flower arrangement, we may expect to see many 'new' kinds in the future. We can assume also, that when we do, the names under which they will be marketed will not be found in any horticultural or botanical dictionary!

The popular use of local names for plants presents many difficulties. Botanical nomenclature, on the other hand, is universally understood. I can only offer a plea to any grower who might be considering marketing and to any collector who is considering exporting perpetuelles, to label them correctly with the aid of a botanist. Even the generic name alone would be more useful and less confusing than some of the names given to these materials.

The flowers which are described botanically in this chapter are well known all over the world. I have been interested to see how universally popular they are, although often they may vary considerably in their deployment.

Seed is available of all those I describe. In the earlier edition of this book I gave cultural directions but I feel that it is not possible nor practical to give detailed cultural directions for every country where this edition might be read. Pondering on this, it occurred to me that it might be most helpful if I were to cite a sample plant. Possibly the most universal flower—which in Britain is grown like the everlastings, as a half-hardy annual—is the so-called African marigold, *Tagetes erecta*, and its many varieties. So my omnibus recommendation is, for the culture of any of the annuals which follow, grow as for tagetes.

*AMMOBIUM ALATUM*, everlasting sand flower, and *A. GRANDIFLORUM* and its varieties, annual.

These are charming little Australian daisies. *A. alatum* is the smaller of the two. They suffer from having large stems in proportion to the size of the blooms. The 2ft tall, branching stems are flattened, much like limonium. Consequently, for many arrangements, the stems need dividing. The short stems can easily be lengthened by inserting wires.

Harvest them as soon as the first blooms open wide. Dry by method 1. Immature buds will not open after drying so it may be best to cut quite short stems, leaving the buds on the plants to develop. Wire the short stems immediately after cutting.

*ANAPHALIS MARGARITACEA* and *A. TRIPLINERVIS*, perennial, the pearly everlasting.

The best species for drying purposes is triplinervis, the

25

leaves of which are downy. To prevent mould, strip the portion of stem where it is to be bound. Take care not to gather the flowers too immature or they will crook badly at the necks. For large decorations whole stems complete with leaves can be used and when this is done it is well worth while taking time to smooth out the dried foliage which becomes creased with drying. Dry by method 1.

*GNAPHALIUM DECURRENS and G. TRINERVE*, two of a species of annuals, perennials and sub-shrubs. The two listed here are good garden plants but there are many other species growing wild in different parts of the world, in America and New Zealand in particular. All would be useful in perpetuelle arrangements. Dry by method 1. Treat as for anaphalis.

*GOMPHRENA GLOBOSA, G. AUREA SUPERBA* and *G. CARNEA,* globe amaranth, globe everlasting, annual.

The first of these is white, red and purple, the second is yellow and the third, flesh pink. The plant originated in India and is to be seen frequently growing in Mediterranean countries, hence one of its popular names, Spanish clover.

The flowers should be cut as soon as the terminal bloom is full grown. This often means sacrificing some of the buds and smaller blooms if the main bloom is to be kept on a stem. Gomphrena takes a long time to dry using method 1. I recommend using method 2 after first wiring the fresh stems.

This flower is useful because it is so different in appearance from the daisylike form of most of the other everlastings. However, the stems are not very robust after drying and subsequently they can be difficult to arrange if they are not reinforced. To wire fresh stems use rose wires which, being dark, are less conspicuous than the fine reel-wire. Insert one end in the stem immediately below the bloom and then gently twist the rest of the wire round the stem to its base. Alternatively, remove the stems leaving an inch or two. The blooms can then be mounted individually or made into clusters, sprays or spikes (see Chapter 10).

HELICHRYSUM. The most widely known and universally used of any species is *Helichrysum bracteatum*, known also as everlasting daisy and strawdaisy. This is an annual, and there are many colours and both dwarf and tall forms. This species is an Australian plant. Others are native to Africa, Europe and the Mediterranean.

The most important thing of all is to gather the blooms at the right time. Don't wait until you see the yellow of their eyes but pick them as soon as you see that they are ready to expand. They will open further when they are dried. If they do not open then they have been gathered too young and if the petals bend back, the blooms have been left too long on the plant. Dry by method 1. Note the comments on beheading the blooms when they are gathered.

It will save time and prove much more convenient in the long run, if the blooms are graded into colour groups, say yellow, orange and red, bronze, crimson and pink and finally white and cream. I like to dry a certain number of buds. Not only do these bring a little more intense colour to an arrangement but they also add interest and variety to it and they will do much to eliminate any stiffness. These can be given graceful arching stems by threading them on false stems of grass (see Chapter 10).

HELIPTERUM, natives of South Africa and Australasia, shrubs, sub-shrubs, perennials and annuals. *Helipterum roseum* synonym *Acroclinium roseum*, Australian everlasting, Immortelle flower, annual.

Another well known strawdaisy and one of the most delightful of all everlastings. The flowers retain their fresh appearance very well after drying. They are also very attractive when used fresh. They can be arranged in water and used again later after drying. The petals are softer in appearance than those of the helichrysum. Their colours are most intense and the centres clearer and better defined when the flowers are gathered soon after they open from the bud stage.

There are many varieties in seed lists and they include double, white, pink and deep rose forms. *H. grandiflorum* is an improved form with large flowers in a variety of white and rose hues. Dry by method 1.

*HELIPTERUM HUMBOLDTIANUM*, annual. This species has bright yellow flowers which grow in clusters some 3 or 4in across. Dry by method 1.

*HELIPTERUM MANGLESII* synonym *Rhodanthe manglesii*, annual, white, pink and rose both single and double forms.

This Australian daisy is very pretty and extremely dainty. It tends to be less manageable than some of the others, mainly because the stems, when fresh, are soft and fleshy and the flowers are borne in drooping clusters loosely spaced out. The stems become very fine when dried and the flowers seem to be more drooping than ever. Of course, this characteristic can be exploited when the flowers are being arranged.

Unless one removes the flowers individually as they mature, which in this case is not really practicable, the stems have to be cut while they still carry many buds. Carefully strip away as much of the foliage as possible without tearing or damaging any side shoots. The leaves will dry dark and become very shrivelled thus giving a shabby appearance to the dried stems. Dry by method 1.

LIMONIUM or statice, mostly annuals or perennials, sometimes sub-shrubs. They grow on sea coasts and salt meadows in all parts of the world. Many are good garden plants.

*Limonium bonduellii* a North African species, perennial but grown as an annual in Britain. The flowers are a good yellow and essential for instilling a little summer sunlight into winter bouquets. *L. sinuatum*, from the Mediteranean, also a perennial grown as an annual. Sometimes called sea lavender because of its colour but seedsmen offer many other hues. Seeds can be bought in separate colours as well as mixed. The blue varieties which have a white 'eye' are lighter and more attractive in appearance than the self colour which tends to become dull when dried.

Both of these may be dried by method 1. Allow the flower spike to mature before it is cut. Those which are too young will never dry properly. Each little bloom in the cluster should be open wide for best results.

*L. suworowii* annual, has pink-lilac thin blooms not unlike an upright *Amaranthus caudatus* or love-lies-bleeding, hence the name candlewick statice. It has a disconcerting habit of drooping these long wick-like inflorescences if they are gathered too immature. It is easy to be misled by the general appearance of the flowers. See that they are open right to the very tips of the inflorescence. Dry by method 2.

All kinds of statice share this characteristic of drooping or wilting badly if they are cut too young. They really should not be dried but at this point it is possible to revive them and then to keep them in water until they have grown more. They can then be dried in the manner prescribed. Stand the stem ends in about 2in of boiling water. Let them

29

remain until the water cools by which time the stems should have become turgid. Place them in fresh, unboiled water with either an added conditioner or a teaspoon of sugar to each pint. Let the flowers remain in this until each floret is mature.

*L. latifolium*, 2-3ft tall, is not unlike perennial gypsophila in appearance but it is a delightful lavender-blue when fresh and well grown. Unfortunately, this colour does not always persist after drying. *L. incana* has the same branching habit but it is shorter, 1½ft, and stiffer in habit. Its white flowers are larger. It is often sold dyed. It can be arranged, like latifolium, right away without preliminary drying.

*LONAS INODORA*, African daisy, annual, the only member of its genus. In spite of its common name it comes from the Mediterranean region.

It is essential that flowers are properly mature before they are gathered. They are tiny yellow button-like blooms in small, dense corymbs. Stems are about 1ft high. Use drying method 1

*XERANTHEMUM ANNUUM* synonym X. *superbissimum*, annual from the Mediterranean and Persia.

The daisy-like flowers are borne on long stems and they vary in colour from white through pink and purple. Seedsmen usually sell them mixed.

There are three varieties of annuum: ligulosum which has semi-double flowers, multiflorum, smaller and more compact generally and perligulosum which has the intriguing description 'very double'. There are also varieties such as album, roseum and purpureum. *X. inapertum* is similar to annuum and has white flowers. Drying method 1 succeeds.

# CHAPTER 3

# These flowers will dry

Most people will, at some time or another, have discovered that the water in a vase has been allowed to dry up and instead of all the flowers dying or dropping as one might have expected, they have instead dried and remained quite recognisable and sometimes quite attractive. This was how I first discovered that delphiniums, pelargoniums and the little pompon chrysanthemums could be used as perpetuelles. If these are given proper treatment they will look so much better than those that have changed their role by accident.

Obviously it would be impossible for me to mention all plants which might produce the right kind of flowers for this purpose and I can only give examples of those I have tried and which I know about. But perhaps the reasons which prompt me to select one rather than another might be of value.

If I notice the slightest tendency on the part of a flower to dry either in the vase or on the plant I then begin to treat it according to one or more of the methods given here. Sometimes this tendency is quite unmistakable. At other times it might be just a hint of an unaccustomed papery texture about the petals.

Most sappy flowers do better dried by the treatment prescribed in method 2 although it does sometimes depend a
little on the season and the climate. If the weather is dry,
warm and not moist and airless, many will dry quickly by
method 1. Examples are *Achillea filipendulina* and *Catananche caerulea*.

One of the problems encountered when planning arrangements is to ensure that there are enough materials for
decorations on a grand scale. Most of the perpetuelles themselves are comparatively small. There are ways and means
of adding both height and mass which I describe later but
it saves a great deal of time, and results in much more effective decorations, if some of the larger plant materials are
dried in quantity.

I was delighted when I discovered that the handsome
spikes of many of the tall border perennials would dry well
and without trouble. Following are some of those found in
most gardens or, in some countries, growing wild.

*ACANTHUS MOLLIS, A. SPINOSUS* and others, Bears
Breeches.

*A. mollis* has white or lilac-pink flowers growing in a long
spike on a 4-5ft stem. *A. spinosus* has erect stems of white
and purple flowers with shiny green bracts.

Gather the spikes when the lowest florets are at their
best; none of them should have faded. If they have, the
spike will not dry a good colour. Try to pick them with as
much of the stem as possible. Later, if necessary, stems can
be made even longer by splicing them to, or mounting
them on, canes.

ACHILLEA. The achillea or yarrow family yields some
useful material. There are many species, some of them with

beautiful silver-grey foliage. The leaves and stems of some of these will dry as will the blooms. The tall yellow variety, *A. filipendulina*, is doubly important because of its erect and sturdy stems 3-4ft high. These toughen on drying and need no wires for support. The dried stems will bend slightly without breaking and this attribute is useful when arrangements are first tied in the hand before being put into narrow-necked containers. (See Chapter 11 and plate p35.)

The flat umbels of flowers retain their shape and solidity and so long as they are gathered at the peak of perfection—just before they reach maturity—they also retain their good colour. This becomes very dull when over-mature flowers are dried. They can be arranged in situ. The seed heads left on the plant are brown and these too retain the attractive flat shape. They look well in both dried and 'wooden' arrangements (see Chapter 10).

The European and British yarrow, *A. millefolium*, both the white and the less common rose, with the garden form Cerise Queen and the American variety lanulosa, will dry well so long as the flowers are mature. Make sure that each floret in the umbel is well formed. If these are too mature the umbels will brown on drying. *A. ptarmica*, or sneeze-wort, has looser heads, the individual white flowers set in attractive corymbs. There are several improved garden varieties. Use method 2 and dry quickly. *A. sibirica* is very similar but of a denser habit with the flower stems more erect and rigid. Perry's White is a fine form of this species. Dry as above.

*ALCHEMILLA MOLLIS*, lady's mantle, perennial.

The delightful cloudlike effect of the masses of the tiny green-yellow flowers can be retained quite successfully. Gather the flowers when they are at their best. Use methods 1 or 2 according to the moisture in the atmosphere. Dryness is more important than speed. The leaves also are worth preserving.

AMARANTHUS, a name which means 'not to wither'.

*A. caudatus*, or love-lies-bleeding, an annual like the rest of the genus, is a plant from the tropics. It is also called chenille and velvet flower. It is particularly useful to the arranger of dried flowers for few other plants give us such graceful pendulous ingredients for perpetuelle decorations. They are especially attractive in wall vases and in pedestal arrangements.

The amaranthus is used as a fresh flower, particularly the green variety, and is often overlooked for drying. The varieties are albiflorus, spikes of which are white or green-white; atropurpureus with blood-red erect spikes, gibbosus a smaller plant altogether with red flowers differently spaced from the others, and viridis which is similar to the first but a strong green.

When well grown the flowers are fat, long and well branched. These generous stems often have to be broken down for easy and effective arrangement. If the plants are grown closer together they will become drawn, and thinner stems with finer spikes will be produced. These will prove more useful for some of the smaller arrangements. The spikes should be gathered as soon as they are ready as those which have become too mature are likely to disintegrate. I prefer to pull up the whole plant by its root and I believe that the blooms dry better this way than when the stems are cut.

There are other species of amaranthus, most of them with many varieties, which have vivid foliage and strange and interesting flowers. All of these will dry and are decorative to a lesser or greater degree. Use method 2.

34

*Page 35*

*(right)* Pressed bracken
fronds, lengthened by
wire mounts, with
*Clematis vitalba* seed
heads, *Briza maxima*,
limonium, anaphalis and
gnaphalium or puatea
(p50)

*(left)* Yellow achillea with
honesty, buff-coloured
saponaria seed heads,
grey-green eucalyptus
leaves and fronds of
yellow chamaecyparis
or false cypress
(p142)

*Page 36* Teasels, lapsana, larch and pressed bracken make a per-manent frame for fresh flowers arranged in water in a small metal cone pushed down below rim level, refreshed when neces-sary. Scarlet anemones are used here (p78)

*CELOSIA CRISTATA* or cockscomb, natives of Asia, Africa and America. It is related to the amaranthus.

There are many handsome varieties, of which *C. cristata pyramidalis* is most useful to the flower arranger. Its flowers grow in a long panicle, often drooping, which is of greater decorative value than the cockscomb-like spike of the species. The colours range from yellow through orange and umber to red and crimson. I find that the orange hues respond best to drying but I have used all of them effectively.

The flowers should be gathered just before they are really mature yet these should not be under-developed or they will not be a good colour or a good shape after drying. Strip the leaves from the stems with care, and dry by method 2. In the case of really large plumes, suspend each stem separately.

*CATANANCHE CAERULEA*, cupid's dart, perennial.

Varieties are alba, white and bicolor, blue and white. There is also a yellow species *C. lutea*.

The flowers are semi-everlasting but they do not always dry successfully. Gather them before they are quite mature and while the colours are still good. Dry by method 2.

*CENTAUREA CYANUS*, cornflower, blue-bottle, annual.

Modern varieties are not only blue but include white, pink, mauve and purple.

I described earlier how these can be dried in a dessicant. They can also be dried by method 1.

Gather the blooms when they are newly opened. Gather buds also at the point when the petals are just protruding from the calyx. These are both pretty and useful for the edges of arrangements. It is most convenient to wire the stems while the flowers are still fresh.

CHRYSANTHEMUMS. Some of the American spray varieties now grown so widely as all-the-year-round types will
dry successfully if merely arranged without water, but only
if they are the tight pompom varieties. Others should be
given an inch of boiling water to begin with and then left
to take it up and dry off slowly. Pompom types from the
garden can often be dried by method 2. The anemone-
centre varieties dry well in dessicants as do the double varieties of *C. maximum.*

*CYNARA CARDUNCULUS,* cardoon, and *C. SCOLYM-
US,* artichoke. The fat thistle-like blooms of both of these
plants should be gathered before they lose their colour. If
left on the plant until the flowers are fertilised they will
later disintegrate in a mass of fluffy seed.

Use either method 1 or 2 according to climatic conditions. If these flowers do not dry properly, mould will spoil
them. If they do become mouldy do not throw them away.
Clean them, dry in a warm cupboard or cooling oven and
use them for brown and 'wooden' arrangements.

DELPHINIUM and LARKSPUR, perennial and annual.
These flowers are both beautiful and varied. I have found
that all will dry, some better or faster than others. Generally speaking the finer spikes with the least sappy stems are
best but there appears to be no firm rule.

Gather the spikes as soon as the top buds are coloured
and before the lowest flower is fully opened if this is possible. Strip the foliage from the stems.

Individual florets cut from the very large spikes make
good focal point flowers in mixed arrangements especially
if they have an 'eye' or a 'bee' centre. These can also be
made into spikes and sprays after drying (see Chapter 10).

I always dry a number of lateral stems of buds, some

green, some slightly coloured. I find these so useful to place at the edges of arrangements where so often some spicate shape is needed and some material other than grasses is called for. Dry by method 2.

ECHINOPS, globe thistle, perennial.

Three species are well known garden plants, *E. bannaticus, ritro* and *sphaerocephalus.* The flowers are blue, silvery grey and almost white. The leaves are downy beneath. These globular blooms will not last well unless they are cut young. Gather them as soon as you see the individual florets opening. Their colour is then at its best.

*ERYNGIUM MARITIMUM,* sea holly, and many other species, perennials mainly.

These flowers are similar in some ways to the echinops but one is from the umbelliferae tribe and the other from the compositae. There are a great many more species than we are likely to see in the average garden. The bracts surrounding the flower heads are often beautifully coloured. They are also often very prickly!

Eryngium can be arranged and left to dry in situ, or by method 1. Gather any of them while they are still young and of a good colour. The much branching stems of some species can be either thinned or divided and it may prove more convenient to attend to some of this before drying, otherwise the bushy stems tend to need a great deal of space.

Individual flowers, the beehive-shaped portion and its collar of bracts, can be mounted by internal wiring and used as a 'bloom' in suitable arrangements.

Eryngium may also be preserved by the glycerine treatment (see Chapter 4). This causes it to turn an attractive brown. Treat mature but not old stems.

*GYPSOPHILA PANICULATA*, chalk plant, perennial.

The large, loose panicles of the tiny flowers, either white or rose, are useful in certain types of arrangements. One should use gypsophila judiciously. For example, this lacy cloud of white or pink will not look so good with dark bronze helichrysums or heavy seed pods of some kinds, yet with soft, silvery pink rhodanthe and white acroclinium it will be very pleasing, and will add a dainty touch to many others.

It is more convenient to divide the wide branching stems before drying. Dry by method 1 until the flowers feel papery and slightly hard to the touch.

HELIANTHUS, annuals and perennials.

Sometimes these dry well. Usually they respond best in dry seasons and the double varieties are better than the single. Use method 2.

LIATRIS, blazing star, button snake-root, North American perennial.

There are several species of liatris which make good garden plants and most will dry. Their tall spikes make them especially useful to the flower arranger. The spicate types begin flowering at the tips, contrary to the way most flowers grow. Gather the flowers while the topmost florets are still at their best and dry by method 2. Spikes which have passed their best are still decorative enough for some purposes although their colour value is not so high.

*MATRICARIA MARITIMA var PLENISSIMA*, double mayweed, annual.

A useful 'filler'. The double daisies are a clear white. Use method 2.

SALVIA, annual, biennial and perennial.

*Salvia splendens* and its varieties, really sub-shrubs but often grown as half-hardy annuals, will dry quite well and keep their colours if not their form. They can be arranged and allowed to dry in situ by either method 1 or 2 and they may also be dried in a dessicant.

Many others of this family will dry well particularly the annual *S. horminum* which grows 18in stems topped by a decorative portion of coloured bracts which are white, violet, dark blue, carmine, purple and violet-blue according to the variety. Dry as for *S. splendens*. The perennial *S. farinacea* which has beautiful spike-like racemes of blue, white or violet flowers, is also well worth drying.

If you like and grow salvias of all kinds, including culinary sage—the purple-foliaged form of which dries well—do experiment. If the flower spikes themselves won't dry, try the seed stems and foliage of others, including the wild plants.

SOLIDAGO, golden rod, perennial.

All the varieties of solidago will dry quite well and keep their form if gathered before the tiny flowers become too developed. On the other hand, they should not be gathered when the flowers are still in bud or newly opened otherwise the 'plumes' shrivel and turn brown. If you wait too long and allow the flowers to mature, even though they may look nice and yellow when you pick them, the seeds will develop and the spikes turn brown and fluffy. Dry quickly using method 2.

*ZINNIA ELEGANS*, annual with many varieties.

A surprising number of these flowers will dry well. Once again, it is the maturity of the bloom at the time it is gathered which is of great importance. All colours do not respond in the same way, yellows, greens and white look most lifelike; reds do not keep good colour.

I recommend putting the flowers in water for a spell to make sure that they are mature before drying them. Begin by standing the stems in boiling water and watch the innermost rays or petals. When these are expanded the flowers can be dried. Zinnias also dry very well in a dessicant, the small and lilliput varieties responding very well and proving most useful in arrangements.

It is advisable to try to wire the blooms as soon as possible after they are gathered; 22 gauge is suitable for the large varieties, 24 gauge for the smaller blooms. Insert the wire from the top down through the centre of the bloom into the hollow stem. This will prevent the neck bending badly as it sometimes does.

UMBELLIFERAE. There are many useful plants belonging to this tribe, and as they mostly resemble each other so closely, I thought it best to group them under the one heading.

Astrantia, masterwort, perennials, and *Didiscus caeruleus*, lace flower, annual, may not at first glance appear to be related but they are and both will dry well.

Astrantia should be gathered as soon as the flowers open if you want to retain the natural colours. Gathered later the whole flower, stem and leaves, will turn varying tones of tan and brown. Use method 2.

Didiscus must be left to open every tiny flower or it will merely shrink on drying. Use method 2. Alternatively use a dessicant but only briefly.

Parsley, chervil, fennel, angelica and other garden herbs from this family, and any of the wild 'Queen Anne's lace' type of flower, should be gathered in their prime and dried by method 1.

Carrot makes a thick umbel of more fibrous growth than those mentioned above. It and any like it are best gathered just as the umbel is beginning to close before going to seed. Dry by method 1 and when dry, gently stroke back the umbels to open them wide again.

## Shrubs whose flowers will dry

ERICA, heather.

Some of the heathers will dry quite well and last a long time before they begin to drop. Much depends upon the stage at which the stems are gathered. Young blooms are more likely to keep their colour than those which are fully developed. Double varieties such as H. E. Beale keep their form best and give a good account of themselves in an arrangement. The spicate shapes are useful as contrast to the rounded daisies. Cut the stems as long as possible, and dry by method 2 or allow to dry in situ.

To prevent the leaves dropping, spray them with a lacquer hair-spray.

HYDRANGEAS. These can be the loveliest of all dried materials and yet to some people they appear to be the most disappointing, judging by the letters I receive. It is all a matter of harvesting. This should not be done until the bracts reach a certain stage. After they have flowered inspect them from time to time.

Perhaps here a little botany would do no harm! Those lovely 'petals' that persist on the hydrangea head and which we try so hard to dry are really not petals at all and do not form a true flower. These are bracts. If you look closely you will see the real flowers, tiny beauties, dainty blue, pink or white according to the colour of the bracts. Hydrangea heads cannot be dried, except in a dessicant, while these

43

little flowers are still alive, nor indeed for some time following their disappearance. As the original colour of the bracts fades, it may be replaced by a much deeper but different one, but the point is that it does change in hue. The bracts might turn just a plain light green according to their environment and to the soil in which the plant is growing. However, with the colour change comes also a change in the tissue of the bracts. These dry out and become somewhat papery. This is a good sign. If the bracts are still fleshy they are not likely to dry without shrivelling badly. Once they become papery and suffused with green or wine and purple go ahead and gather them.

I have left them on the bush right through winter and picked them at Christmas but, generally speaking, they are best gathered for drying before the frost affects them. Dry by method 2.

**LAVENDER.** When you consider how much is dried and used for other purposes it is surprising how seldom lavender is used in mixtures of dried flowers.

The best types for drying are those which are deepest in colour because all tend to fade. However, much of the colour is retained and a little of the essential fragrance lingers on. The flower spikes should be gathered soon after they open. Inspect the spike to ensure that the topmost flowers are open. Too young spikes will droop. Dry by method 2.

**MIMOSA, wattle.** This pretty blossom will keep for months when dried and if you have some in a fresh flower arrangement which has lost its fluffiness, simply set it aside for perpetuelle decoration. Usually, it is best to remove the leaves but this really depends upon whether they are large or small.

The tiny yellow blobs of bloom make good contrasts with brown spikes and rounded seed leaves. The fern-like leaves of some mimosas last well. They may also be pressed. Dry by method 2.

PROTEA. That wonderful African plant family Protea-ceae provides a fabulous store of strange and extremely handsome flowers, foliage and seed cases. Vaguely resembling artichokes, protea blooms can be both used and dried in much the same manner. (See plate p71.)

Proteas, both dried and fresh, are imported by many countries and they grow also in tropical and semi-tropical surroundings. The blooms vary according to the species, some being small enough for an average sized arrangement while others are very large. Some come as heads only with a very short stem butt which has to be mounted, but others come on good stems with foliage attached. Dry by method 2. The foliage is also sold separately, as is the ready-dried cup-shaped involucre of bracts which is often trimmed to bring the head down to a size roughly equal to a medium zinnia (which it resembles) and sold as sun-scorched protea. It is a rich brown and resembles a flower made from slicing a cone.

The so-called sugar bush stars are the flowers from *P. mellifera* which are 4in long, cup-shaped and 3in wide.

ROSES. As I write, in early spring, there is a little bunch of tiny rosebuds nearby, pink and perfect in their way, quite dry and yet looking as though they would open with the slightest coaxing. These were gathered in January, mid-winter. I happened to see them on the bushes and brought them in to dry.

At one time I used to suggest that only the double forms of roses, the ramblers, moss and the old-fashioned kinds, whose petals grow a little papery with age, should be dried but I have since found that many of the modern hybrids will respond well to all methods of drying. I have found also that much depends upon the time of year when they are gathered and it seems that those which are picked when growth is slower, late autumn rather than summer for instance, dry better and quicker than those cut at other times.

Some varieties and some colours do much better than others, pale tints being better than deep reds. Sometimes the rose dries and keeps its shape beautifully but its petals turn brown. Such flowers look well in 'wooden' arrangements and they can also be sprayed with gold paint—very lightly—and used for party decorations. Dry by method 2.

WISTERIA and LABURNUM. If you hope to make some outsize arrangements gather branches of these blossoms when they are at their best. Dry by method 1 unless the air is too moist, in which case switch to method 2.

## Pressing flowers

There are some flowers that may be successfully pressed. These then hold their colour and although they may not hold their shape in the dry atmosphere of a room, they will look well assembled in a plaque arrangement or mounted on a calendar or a wall picture.

Faced flowers, those which can be flattened fairly easily, such as violas, florets of hydrangeas, thin daisies or primroses, for example, are best. When the blooms are being prepared for pressing see that the petals overlap flatly and that none is bent the wrong way.

One of the best ways to press and dry quickly is to cover the flowers with sand and leave this open to the air in a warm dry place.

# CHAPTER 4

# Foliage and ferns

Those who have to buy the foliage for their flower arrangements will discover that there are now many kinds on sale, some home grown and some imported, and this applies to most countries. There are aspidistra, broom, cycas, cecropia, eucalyptus, ficus, grevillea, mahonia, macadamia, magnolia and palmetto as well as ferns of all kinds, all either dried or preserved in some way. Even so, I think that the greatest satisfaction which comes from making dried flower arrangements is gained from collecting one's own material and processing it at home.

## The glycerine method

One of the best ways of preserving whole branches is by the glycerine method, ie in a solution made of one-third glycerine, two-thirds water, as follows: place 2in of the stems in the mixture and let them stand in it until you can see traces of glycerine in the leaves which will become silkier and a little oilier. Often you can see the veins turn a deeper colour and from them you can watch the solution spread throughout the leaf. When enough has been taken, remove the stems from the solution, otherwise the leaves are likely to begin exuding the oil.

While I find it impossible to give hard and fast rules covering every kind of leaf, here are a few tips. Never attempt to preserve by the above method branches that do not take up water properly when they are normally arranged. You will be wasting your time. In any case, always begin by standing all branches overnight in plain water, first heated to 70°F. Slit the stem ends before putting the branches in water. This need not be a deep drink but 2in at least of the stem end should be under water. If by the morning some branches have failed to take water and show this by curling leaves, reject them. Foliage known to be difficult is best stood in 2in of boiling water and left until it is obvious that the leaves are turgid and taking water.

As a rule, I find that most smooth leaves may be preserved this way while rough leaves may not. Do not confuse rough with downy for many of these take the glycerine solution well.

When mixing the water and glycerine, boil the water and add it to the latter. I find it best to use jars and tins to hold the branches and other stems and, because they become top-heavy, I place each inside a deeper, wider vessel. This way, less solution is needed.

## Leaves that will dry green

Most evergreens can be dried and will keep both their colour and form. The most lifelike after drying are those which grow flat or which can easily be flattened.

After gathering, wash them well to remove grime. To do this, swish them round in luke warm water containing detergent. Drain the branches on newspaper holding the stems down with a weight where necessary.

48

When they are quite dry, lay them between sheets of newspaper fixing them with adhesive tape in places should this be necessary, to keep them flat. Weight them down in some way—a slab of marble, a layer of sand, several bricks or books are some of the things you can use. Let them stay this way for at least a month.

To dry branches so that they are not pressed too flat, this applies to those which did not grow flat in the first place, arrange them on sheets of newspaper as described above and stack them, separating each branch from the sheet above it with a buffer in the form of a thick paper towel, napkin or blotting paper. Make them into a parcel by placing a piece of cardboard under the lowest sheet and on the top one. This should overlap the newspaper sheets. Tie the bundle with string to hold all in place and put a light weight on top.

## Pressing individual leaves and branches

Some leaves do not satisfactorily respond to the glycerine treatment; they may take the fluid quite well but one is not able to fix the leaf colour or discover a new one. Instead of the delightful hues present in the leaves at the time, as there are in so many of them in the fall, the leaves turn instead to a dull uninteresting hue.

Almost all these autumn-tinted branches can be pressed. After pressing they will keep their shape and form. If some seem too stiff, take time and curl some of the leaves slightly.

Pressing individual leaves is a little more fussy and calls for more patience than preserving them. Sometimes the process can be hastened by ironing—this also helps to fix the colour in some cases. Cut the leaves as soon as they have turned colour and on a dry day. Using a hot iron and a newspaper as an ironing pad, press the leaves one by one.

49

Lay a tissue over each to absorb moisture and also to protect the iron from becoming stained or sticky.

After pressing, finish drying the leaves by placing them between pages of a magazine. Put this under a good weight. They should be ready in about two weeks but they can be left longer quite safely.

## *Pressing ferns*

Probably the most popular fern in permanent decoration is the bracken. It is so common and also so much of a pest in many areas that one need have no compunction about advising its use and suggesting that plenty is taken.

Bracken fronds should be gathered early in the season and while they are still flat. They are flat because they still hold sap. Once this stops flowing the fronds start to curl. Unfortunately, the curl is not beneficial for it clouds the beauty of the frond instead of enhancing it and any attempted arrangement of these curly fronds results in a bird's nest effect. It is possible to collect a whole range of bracken hues with ferns coloured from almost white to a deep burnt sienna. (See plate p35.)

Bracken can be pressed and it is as good preserved this way as any although some people immerse the fronds in the hot glycerine solution. I don't like this method because the fern looks oily. To press, take care that the fronds are laid flat, well spaced and not one on another or they will stick together. It is best to lay a sheet of newspaper between each. It is also often more convenient to cut the large lateral or side fronds from the main stem rather than to attempt to press a great piece. Many laterals are quite large.

All green ferns may be pressed and they will stay green and keep their shape after arrangement. It is also possible to stand the fronds in the glycerine solution for a short time, two or three days, to preserve them for some weeks. Alternatively, they may be stood in the solution and then pressed.

I cannot possibly list all the foliage that can be either preserved by glycerine or pressed but here follows a list of some of the best known with which I have experimented and used during the past decade.

ACER (maple). Among the many maples are some of the loveliest and most useful leaves for the flower arranger. Unfortunately, none that I know take glycerine well and I find that whole branches are more successfully dried by pressing. If they are pressed as soon as they change colour in the autumn, they will hold the hue well and, what is more, will retain their leaves. If the season is advanced before they are pressed most of the leaves will fall after drying.

It is sometimes possible to coax the stems to take the solution by first completely immersing the branches in water for at least three hours, and then standing the stem ends in the hot glycerine solution.

In summer, branches of the small-leaved species and varieties should be gathered while they are at their prime and pressed between newspaper under a shallow layer of sand. At the same time and also in autumn, press large maple leaves of all kinds. These will prove invaluable later on.

ASPIDISTRA. Green leaves can be given glycerine solution but they should be mature. (No young leaves take the solution well.) Arrangers may not have enough plants to be able to gather green leaves in any numbers but it is worth noting that any leaf which has turned brown at the tip, indicating that it has begun to fade, can be cut from a pot plant and stood in solution.

Any leaves which have faded on a plant should be cut and saved. These can be bleached or used as they are. To induce the leaves to curl, roll them up from tip to stem, tie round the centre with a thread to keep the roll tight, and store. Uncurl when required.

CAMELLIA. Sprays of camellia foliage can be stood in a glycerine solution. This should be done as soon as possible after cutting otherwise the leaves may drop badly. (Do not throw away any preserved leaves which fall. These can be mounted individually and used in many types of arrangement.)

The deep green leaves change to a leather-brown and are among the most attractive of all preserved foliage. Remove the branches from the solution once the leaves have changed colour. If they are left in it too long this also can cause leaf drop.

CONIFERS. The arranger of dried flowers is inevitably involved in Christmas decorations and many of the perpetuelles look well in seasonable garlands, swags, ropes and other designs.

Being Christmas it is essential that they should contain one or more evergreens either for backing or for applied decoration. Fortunately, most of the plants in the great conifer group dry well. Some, such as yew, last only for a few weeks unless they have been treated previously with glycerine (when they become everbrown and not evergreen) but others last several months.

Where only deep green conifers are required, the problem of dropping needles is often a vexing one. A plastic transplanting spray material is available which can be useful in helping to retain needles which might otherwise fall from cut boughts. Sprays of this kind are used by some

*Page 53*

Wire-netting tops
dry Oasis to hold
stems of oats, phy-
salis, sycamore keys
and mahonia foli-
age; preserved oak
fills in lower back-
ground, more keys
and shorter stems
of physalis are
arranged at rim
level; a fan-shaped
piece of larch fits
neatly at the back
and fills the space
between physalis
and oak without
dominating them.
Physalis at the rim
level are opened to
reveal the bright
berry within
(p85)

*Page 54* A silver birch container, packed with dry Oasis, holds
*Iris sibirica*, clematis and centaurea seed heads, acroclinium,
carthamus, honesty, hydrangea and olearia, grevillea, senecio
and thuja foliage (p95)

plantsmen to protect certain trees and shrubs from trans-
piration losses during planting. The spray, applied under
pressure, covers the entire plant with a wax-like film which
is almost invisible and which falls away and disappears after
a few weeks.

The best naturally drying pine I have found so far is the
blue cedar but there may be others I have not yet handled.
This one retains its needles and lasts from one year to the
next if it is carefully stored. It will dry in situ and needs no
special treatment. I find that decorations made the previous
year and carefully stored are usually intact the following
year although the colour is faded. A little freshener of a
spray of paint and a sprinkling of glitter makes them smart
again.

Many of the more fern-like conifers are attractive in
other types of decorations than those used solely at Christmas. I search for blue-grey and golden varieties of chamaecyparis, thuja and others to arrange with flowers and other
types of perpetuelles. Their tiny cones often produced over
the surface of the foliage are also well worth using. These
all dry well and can be arranged fresh and left to dry in the
arrangement.

CYCAS (palm). Leaves of this palm have been a favourite
of florists for a long time and are used mostly in funeral
tributes of all kinds. I saw their possibilities as a material
for perpetuelle arrangements when I first became interested in this form of floristry and I used them first, painted
and glittered, in Christmas decorations (see plate p108).

They are marketed ready preserved in some way and then
treated with a type of varnish. This gives them a glossy
green, highly polished and unnatural appearance. Bleached
cycas leaves are also available. The leaves are usually sold
in bundles and are obtainable in various lengths from

about 6in to nearly 3ft. Thus there are cycas 'fronds' for use in almost any kind of arrangement.

*CARPINUS BETULUS*, hornbeam. If you can gather some of the branches complete with the 'keys' these also can be preserved by the glycerine method. The earlier in the season, ie summer, the leaves are preserved the deeper will be the ultimate colour. For autumn tints, begin to pick the branches when you see one or two showing colour on the tree. Do not wait until the entire tree is coloured.

**CASTANEA**, sweet chestnut. Branches of leaves which are only just beginning to turn colour can be pressed. If these are left too long on the trees the leaves are apt to fall after pressing. Branches gathered early in the season can be preserved by the glycerine method but they will not become the characteristic tan in colour.

Individual leaves are often very useful. These may be gathered from the trees or picked up from beneath it. Press them if you wish them to keep their flat surface but often the slight curl that comes with drying in the air is more attractive.

**COTONEASTER**. Most kinds can be preserved by the glycerine method.

**ELAEAGNUS**. Preserve by glycerine method. Leaves become golden-brown in about six weeks.

**EUCALYPTUS**. This beautiful evergreen is well worth growing or buying for preservation alone. In fact, the branches dry quite well without treatment but they then have that inevitable dehydrated look about them. A more lively look can be given them by using the glyerine solution

but in a slightly different way. You can get foliage of varying tones by standing some branches in the solution for
twenty-four hours, others for a few days and so on. I have
always found the short period of treatment worth giving
even for preserving stems for arranging with fresh flowers.
The short spell in the solution does not appear to effect the
soft and lovely grey of the leaves.

The orange and coral coloured flower buds often present
on bought eucalyptus also dry well and with no special
treatment. They can be arranged and left to dry in situ.

*EUPHORBIA MARGINATA.* This pretty variegated annual spurge dries beautifully in a dessicant. The striking
stem tops of leaves can play the role of a bloom in a centre
of a large arrangement.

*FATSIA JAPONICA.* The large palmate leaves of this
evergreen are both extremely handsome and very useful for
really large arrangements. Mature leaves can be preserved
by the glycerine method; fallen leaves which have not yet
become brittle can be treated in two ways. They can be
oiled—olive oil is good for this purpose and this will clean
the leaves as well as make them supple; or they can be
bleached.

FAGUS, beech. As the summer draws to its close many
people resolve to preserve some beech for autumn and winter decoration. Alas, the resolution is often made too late.
The trees are already golden and the first thin carpets of
fallen leaves lie round their trunks like little pools of light.
To capture this golden spirit of the fall you should usually
make your preparations early while the leaves, or the major-
ity of them, are still green.

Leaves gathered from July onwards can be preserved by

the glycerine method. At this early stage they will turn a dark hue not unlike the copper beech. If the branches are picked complete with the beech-mast, the preservative will fix these also. They will open out and look like little starry four-petalled flowers. The nuts remain packed tightly together in a little pointed centre. As the season passes leaves will be lighter and lighter after preservation.

**HEDERA**, ivy. Immerse the trails or individual leaves in glycerine solution for a week to ten days.

*HELLEBORUS CORSICUS*. Wait until the leaves are tough and mature and preserve in glycerine.

**ILEX**, holly. Since one of the beauties of holly is that it is so evergreen, readers may not be interested in the fact that it can be preserved by the glycerine method, but glossy brown holly leaves do look well in swags and garlands made after the style of the Grinling Gibbons carvings.

Variegated holly, particularly the silver varieties rather than the gold, will also dry fairly well either in sprigs or as individual leaves. (See plate p90.)

**LAUREL**, see Prunus.

**LAURUS**, bay. Dry by hanging. Preserve by glycerine method. Leaves will turn a deep brown.

**MAHONIA**. The foliage of *M. aquifolium*, synonym *Berberis aquifolium*, often becomes beautifully coloured in winter. Individual but compound leaves can be lightly pressed and will still keep most of their colour. They can also be arranged in situ with no special treatment but this sometimes results in the colour fading fast. Alternatively, the leaves can be lightly oiled or sprayed with a colourless lacquer.

Sometimes you will find a whole stem will dry splendidly but the surest way is to use the glycerine method in the manner prescribed for eucalyptus. The very tip of an attractively coloured stem will usually keep its colour without any special treatment and it can be used first in a fresh flower arrangement and later dried.

All the mahonias and berberis respond to various ways of preservation but be wary of the very spiny kinds of the latter which often can be more of a nuisance than a help. Lightweight materials tend to get caught in the spines and easily moved out of place.

The foliage of *M. napaulensis* and *bealeii* often turn glorious red and corn yellow in autumn and winter. These leaves can be cut and used right away. They need no particular treatment. As they age they become matt in appearance. If this is not pleasing, they can be sprayed with lacquer or lightly oiled.

MAGNOLIA. I have already described how the fallen magnolia leaves can be skeletonised. They can also be cleaned and oiled in the same way as fatsia. Green, mature leaves, either individual or on branches, can be preserved by the glycerine method. They become a rich chestnut-brown in about six weeks.

*OSMUNDA REGALIS*, royal fern. These can be pressed as described earlier. Fronds which have dried naturally on the plant are usually perfectly all right for decoration. Gather them before the frost touches them.

OLEANDER, *Nerium oleander*. Branches of this lovely flowering shrub can be dried. Select only those which have

59

not flowered and gather them when the foliage is mature and not new and soft. Dry by method 1.

PAEONY. Mature foliage and young seed pods attached can be preserved by using the glycerine method.

*PRUNUS CERASIFERA*, cherry laurel; *P. LUSITAN-ICA*, Portugal laurel. Any evergreen prunus can be preserved by the gycerine method. Gather mature, not young, growths. The leaves turn a handsome, leathery brown.

QUERCUS, oak. All species of oak preserve well by the glycerine method. The gnarled branches offer a pleasant change from the smooth outlines of most of the others. These look well in silhouette but, like many other subjects, some of the leaves may need removing either because they are damaged in some way or because they grow too thickly.

Deciduous kinds should be gathered immediately the branches begin to change colour on the tree. At this point the veins will still be green in most species. Tough fallen leaves can be skeletonised

The beautiful red species and varieties do not retain their colours after preservation.

ROSA, rose. Some rose species foliage, omoiensis for instance, and others which have tiny, tough leaves and non-succulent stems, can be dried by method 1 and also preserved in glycerine. In each case, gather mature growths only.

RUBUS, raspberry. The backs of the leaves of many of this family are silvery. The leaves can be pressed quite effectively. When displayed they should be shown with the silvery sides uppermost.

RUSCUS or butcher's broom. The butcher's broom is an odd, prickly little shrub sometimes used with dried flowers but more often in Christmas decorations when it is silvered, gilded or bleached.

RHODODENDRON. I seem to use more rhododendron leaves than any other kind of foliage. These are mostly fallen leaves which I gather while walking round some great garden or arboretum. Fortunately, no one minds fallen leaves being picked up and taken away. They vary considerably. The flower arranger would be wise to study the undersides of all of them. Some are soft, silvery grey, others handsomely felted in warm orange and rust. Some are long and pointed, just the thing for placing at the edges of arrangements or to taper the ends of a swag. There are some which are quite small and others which are enormous.

Fallen leaves need no special treatment. You can simply mount them and use them right away. If you have reason to believe that they need cleaning treat them as fatsia.

SABAL, palm and palmetto. The leaves of both greenhouse and outdoor palms can be preserved by the glycerine treatment. Faded leaves which have dried naturally on the plant can also be used. Treat as for fatsia. Some arrangers like to trim these by cutting the tips of the fronds level. I don't do this myself but I have seen trimmed leaves used very effectively, especially in arrangements designed for contemporary settings.

*SAXIFRAGA umbrosa*, London pride. Whole rosettes of this plant can be used in the same way as if each was a flower. Gather those which are of good colour, dry by method 1 and mount on wire stems for arrangement. They can also be preserved by the glycerine method when they will turn a dark brown.

**SELAGINELLA.** Grown in greenhouses in cool climates, this is a tropical plant allied to the ferns. The trails are extremely graceful, and can be used immediately after cutting; they will dry in situ.

*VIBURNUM TINUS, V. RHYTIDOPHYLLUM.* The leaves of the first species can be preserved by glycerine solution. The second shrub grows untidily and its entire branches are seldom suitable for arrangements. However, its dark evergreen leaves with their attractive mealy undersides will last well and are useful when large arrangements have to be made. Either hang them to dry or use them right away.

**VITIS,** vine. Autumn-tinted vine leaves can be pressed and they will keep their colours fairly well. The great disadvantage is that they become very brittle and must therefore be handled very gently. For this reason it is best to mount the leaves on false stems before pressing them (see Chapter 10). Keep the leaves inside the pressing papers, the stems out.

When they are dry, the pressed leaves can be lightly oiled to give them an attractive gleam; alternatively lay them in oil for a while for this is likely to be a very delicate operation if you are to avoid shattering the leaf. Spraying the surface with a light lacquer is quite effective. Hair-spray gives a little more body to the leaf.

Individual sprays as well as leaves of the downy kinds such as the Dusty Miller grape should be gathered in late summer and pressed.

# Silver or grey-leaved plants

The silver-leaved plants dry well. Individual leaves of some kinds are best pressed. In some cases the whole rosette of a plant can be used in much the same way as a bloom. Some of these can be mounted on false stems and arranged right away but most of them will be improved by a little preliminary drying either by method 2 or by a short period in a dessicant.

In some cases the flowers and the flower spikes are worth drying. Such a plant is *Stachys lanata*. Leaves, young woolly flower spikes and whole leaf clusters can be used. Leaves are best first mounted on wires and then pressed or ironed.

Verbascum can be used in much the same way. Those with the most downy leaves are *V. bombicyferum* and glaucium. *V. broussa* has a particularly lovely woolly stem. Glycerine can be used for stems and large leaves. The colour becomes several tones deeper and the shading is quite interesting. Gather the flowering stems after the blooms have mainly finished but before they are touched with frost.

The shrubby senecios are very beautiful when their flower stems are in tight silver buds. I like to gather these (the bush meanwhile is improved for not being allowed to flower) and dry them by method 1. Individual leaves of the same plant are pressed.

Some leaves are silvery only on the undersides, and generally speaking, these come from larger shrubs or—in the case of some of the maples—from trees. *Buddleia globosa* has attractive leaves of this kind. *Grevillea robusta*, with graceful, strap-like serrated-edged leaves, the silk oak, is another charming, slightly silvered plant. Like the eucalyptus, this is another Australian plant and so one assumes that it can be grown in any climate where the former is to be seen.

## FOLIAGE AND FERNS

Bunches of the foliage are often to be seen on sale, both fresh and dyed. The latter keep their form better than the untreated ones, but any of them can be ironed or otherwise pressed back into shape. Fresh foliage can be dried by method 1 or treated with glycerine in the same way as described for eucalyptus.

I use a lot of grevillea because there is nothing else that I know of quite the same graceful character. The stems are long and, although the foliage grows upwards, fairly bushy. I like to divide the stems quite considerably, removing the largest leaves and arranging them individually. These leaves have lovely outlines and they are long and slender. They are perfect for adding contrast to the numerous rounded forms present in so many perpetuelles.

# CHAPTER 5

# Grasses and sedges

Many arrangers are rediscovering the decorative beauty and value of grasses, fresh, dried, native and imported. As ingredients in some mixed arrangements or merely as combinations with another material they are irreplaceable. Often grass only, provided that it is the right kind of grass, will furnish that suggestion of curve, that hint of extra height or width or that faint but much needed suggestion of grace.

Although so many lovely native species may be gathered from the fields and hedgerows the choicest are not always found easily. Grasses are, however, easy to grow, and seed is readily obtainable.

## Cereals

Before we discuss the ornamental grasses let us not forget those which, although grown primarily for food, are among the loveliest of them all. Wheat, barley, oats and millet, sturdy straight-stemmed materials, can provide that little extra height so often necessary for perfect balance. They are invaluable also for arrangements which have to be made larger than life, in which case they can often be made into simple sheaves and mounted on long, false stems. (See plate p 00.)

Wheat is perhaps a little stiff, but even so it has its part to play and it is surprising how, merely by turning a stem so that it flows in the direction of the slightest curve in the seedhead, one can break down any rigidity and give instead a hint of movement.

Oats are tall and graceful and we should include also the animated oats, *Avena sterilis*, which gardeners grow as an ornamental grass.

I like barley best of all, because of its long graceful beard which satisfies my liking for sweeping lines and etched effects. The seedhead is often placed at an attractive angle to the stem, a good point where mainly stiff stems are used as they so frequently are in perpetuelle arrangements.

Oats, wheat and barley are not so satisfying arranged in a mixture since each seems to rob the other of its character but used individually as a complement to certain other materials they are lovely indeed. Alternatively, if used together in an arrangement they should be grouped in their kinds rather than mixed. For example, the severe, untrammelled stems of wheat should be placed in the centre of the materials, the barley to one side, its lines flowing outwards, away from the central wheat, and on the other side the oats, curving away from the centre.

One can buy bleached and dyed barley and very lovely some of it is too. In some countries it is possible to buy the other cereals. These are usually dried and sometimes bleached.

You can hold some of the green in cereals if you gather them early before the seed is ripe and dry them by method 1.

## Straws

Grasses can be of value in many ways, not least because they provide straws. In this context, the term 'straw' is used to describe any grass stem without its inflorescence. If, during the summer, good fat bunches of all kinds of grasses are gathered, arrangers will have a sufficiency of stems for many types of perpetuelles. For instance, straws saved from the stems of the thick grasses and cereals will make good false stems for some of the heavier materials and largest flowers. If necessary, they can always be reinforced by inserting wires. The more graceful stems can support the small blooms and will eliminate the stiffness which comes from all wire stems.

It is often quite simple and extremely effective to mount a false stem on a leaf, flower or some other item merely by inserting the short petiole into the straw. Sometimes the base of the stem may be swollen, as it is in leaves for instance, in which case the base may have to be tapered. As a precaution this stem base can be given the slightest touch of adhesive. I have much more to say about mounting in Chapter 10.

Almost all countries are rich in grasses of some kind or another. I cannot list all the grasses which are suitable but I can say that if a grass is pretty in life it is almost certain to be attractive when dried. I must repeat, grasses should be gathered early when their colour is best, often before the inflorescence has completely left its sheath. This can be stripped away later. They should then be dried slowly and away from light.

Among the grasses which I have found most useful are the following.

*AIRA ELEGANS* or hair grass is extremely dainty. *A*.

*Pulchella* is a little heavier in appearance. Both are annuals.

*ALOPECURUS LANATUS* lamb's tail grass. Its inflorescence is soft and woolly as its name implies. It is perennial.

*ANTHOXANTHUM ODORATUM*, sweet vernal grass, with the odour of new mown hay, is also perennial.

*AVENA STERILIS*, or animated oat, has awns or bristle-like appendages which are susceptible to changes of weather and become animated. There are other oats, annual or perennial. Most are attractive in some way or another.

*AGROSTIS ALBA*, fiorin has cloudy white plumes which are very dainty indeed. *A. nebulosa* is known as cloud grass. Both are annuals.

*BRIZA MAXIMA* or pearl grass, often on sale, has large flat locket-shaped inflorescences and is one of the most handsome of all the cultivated grasses. It grows from 12in to 15in high, taller than most. *Briza Gracilis*, quaking grass, is smaller and quite unlike any other grass. There are other quaking grasses, both annual and perennial species.

*BROMUS BRIZIFORMIS*, an annual, brome grass is, for most people, a typical 'grass'. There are many species.

*BRACHYPODIUM DISTACHYON*, false brome grass, is an annual often cultivated in gardens.

*CORTADERIA RUDIUSCULA*, *C. selloana*, pampas grass, perennial, can contribute most handsomely to large

68

perpetuelle decorations. The tall handsome plumes are perfect in large or outsize decorations and one should bear in mind when planning these that the long stem is responsible for the pleasing proportions. Once the stem is cut short the grass becomes somewhat overbearing. This grass is sold either natural or dyed.

*COIX LACRYMA-JOBI,* job's tears, a most beautiful annual species of tropical Asia. This was once a great favourite with Victorian ladies and was much cultivated for the decorative beauty of its pearly grey inflorescences. The grass grows 2-3ft high. The leaves are thick and resemble those of maize. There is a variegated form *C. aurea zebrina.*

*ERIANTHUS RAVENNAE,* ravenna grass or woolly beard grass, perennial, is not unlike the pampas in appearance. It is a garden plant, and is on sale in most florists' shops both in its natural state and dyed.

The plumes may be used as they are on long stems, like the pampas or they can be thinned out or divided. Short thinnings can be used in smaller designs. They can be raised by false stems of straw.

*HORDEUM JUBATUM,* squirrel tail grass, annual, is a native of North America. It grows about 2ft high so, apart from its lovely plumes or tails, it is a welcome addition to an arrangement. It must be cut young otherwise the tails will disintegrate.

*LAGURUS OVATUS,* hare's tail grass, annual, is one of the prettiest of the European species. Its inflorescences are soft and fluffy. One should use them discreetly in arrangements otherwise they tend to give a furry impression to the whole.

69

*STIPA PENNATA*, feather grass, *S. elegantissima*, perennials, are both garden plants. They become ornamented with several delicate arching stems 2ft high or so, each festooned with soft, waving, style-like streamers resembling in some ways the tail of a bird of paradise.

ZEA, maize. There are several decorative forms of zea which are useful to the flower arranger, including the strawberry popcorn which really does resemble a strawberry in many ways, and the enormous various-coloured 'Squaw' corn. The ordinary sweet corn can be used as giant 'blooms'. The husks should be pulled back from the corn and turned into 'petals' to make corn-cob daisies. Varieties with short cobs are best.

Sweet corn can be made into swags (see Chapter 10). The outer husks, which are tough and papery can be coiled into 'roses'.

## Reeds and Sedges

More and more, among the perpetuelles offered for sale, one sees many species of reeds and sedges and I imagine we can hope to see even more as time goes on. The most familiar of all must surely be the giant reed-mace, cat-tail or bulrush, the favourite of Victorian arrangers!

*TYPHA LATIFOLIA*, which grows 6ft to 8ft high, is suitable only for very tall arrangements yet one often sees it in small decorations where it looks thoroughly out of place and out of proportion. There are smaller species: *T. mimina* for instance grows from 12in to 18in high. Many of the smaller kinds are on sale. These are usually a pleasant light brown in colour and not much thicker than a pencil. Sometimes they are called pencil-rushes.

*Page 71*

*(left)* 'Sun-scorched'
protea, larch and
pine cones, lupin,
antirrhinum and
sedum seed heads,
hydrangea rushes,
sweet chestnut burrs,
beech, eucalyptus
and cryptomeria
foliage (p45)

*ht)* Two large car-
e and smaller
thamus thistles,
h nicandra,
rangea, larch,
at, leonotis,
emocarpus and
*sibirica* seed
ds, cryptomeria
es, fungi 'flow-
, beech and
nder foliage
7)

*Page 72* Grevillea and eucalyptus foliage, hypericum seed heads, anaphalis, helipterum, fungi 'flowers', cryptomeria cones and two cone 'roses' made from small cones for centres and large cone scales for 'petals' (p100)

The most important thing to bear in mind is to gather the rush while it is young. Take care also that you do not handle the plush part for this may cause it to disintegrate. Cat-tails or bulrushes can be arranged right away. They need no special treatment.

JUNCUS. There are several species of rushes, true rushes, which are pretty enough to be included in dried arrangements. Most of them are 2ft high or so.

CYPERACEAE. In this family lies a wealth of material for drying, from the dainty cotton-grass through the sedges both small and dainty and large and handsome. They are too numerous to list separately. All should be gathered just as they become mature, and dried by method 1.

# CHAPTER 6

# Seed heads and flower skeletons

If you are interested in form, line or pattern, this division of the perpetuelle materials will bring you endless pleasure. Arrangements of seed structures, placed against the right background, can be the softest, most soothing piece of furniture in the room. On the other hand they can be the most exciting.

Seed vessels vary considerably, as much as the flowers themselves. Outstanding examples will be described later but I would like to draw your attention to most members of the lily tribe which will produce very handsome pods. It may be bad gardening not to remove the seed pods as soon as the petals have faded but to make amends, you will have some strong, long-lasting perpetuelles. Many of these are on sale and they include such items as yucca and its near relation, agave. These are tough in texture and wooden in appearance.

After the flower has ripened and given place to the seed vessel, the plant tissues change and become more woody. Some become brittle and are obviously not much use unless they can be handled with the greatest care, but others are really tough and will last for years. The range of texture, like that of form, seems inexhaustible.

I like to collect some of the green unripe kinds and treat them in two ways. Some I dry slowly by method 1 to give me some green hues later. As a rule I choose hollow types, not succulents, for this: aquilegia and poppies for instance. The others are stood in the glycerine solution. Most will turn colour, some of them quite soon, but others take several weeks. It is really well worth while experimenting with the latter process for one gets some lovely and often unexpected results.

Dried seed stems can usually be bleached quite effectively in the same way as described for leaves. Many bleached kinds are on sale but it seems to me that these are often over bleached and need a little more light and shade to them.

ALLIUM. Many plants of the onion tribe, both culinary and decorative, produce attractive globular flowers which leave behind them some of the most beautiful of all the seed heads. Gather them when the individual seed vessels are swollen with almost ripe seed and almost touching each other. Dry by method 1.

*ANGELICA ARCHANGELICA* is something for those who want to make large arrangements. The seed heads are globose. Gather them when they are newly matured for if the seed is ripe you will not retain the dense globe. Dry by method 1. Other members of the umbelliferae also produce handsome seed heads not as rounded as the angelica but still worth saving in the same way.

*AQUILEGIA*, columbine, seed heads are beautifully shaped. They can be gathered green or let dry naturally on

75

the plant. If they are to be picked green, give them time to grow to a good size. They can be arranged right away and left to dry in the arrangement, or they can be hung and dried. They may also be preserved in glycerine solution. Treat tall seeded stems and their attached leaves. Both turn to good tan tones.

*ATRIPLEX HORTENSIS*, or mountain spinach, orach, an annual which has attractive varieties with beautifully coloured foliage. The value of these varieties to the arranger of dried flowers lies in their long seed stems. These should be gathered young and dried by method 1. The red stems become tan-coloured.

*CAMPANULA MEDIUM*, canterbury bells, leave behind them some enchanting seed cases frilled with scalloped edges. These can be gathered green and dried by method 1. They can also be left to ripen thoroughly on the plant and then skeletonised in the same way as leaves. Occasionally, one finds naturally skeletonised seed cases on the plant in winter. These usually need to be washed and just slightly bleached.

COMPOSITAE. The daisy family contains many plants which have interesting and often surprisingly beautiful seed structures. Of course, those wonderful stand-bys, the helichrysums and helipterums, are members of this family but these are flowers proper and not the cases which held them or were once part of them.

The daisy is not one flower but, as its tribe name indicates, several florets all radiating from the centre ring of more florets which make up the 'eye'. Such closely packed members need a strong and sturdy case to hold them firm, and in almost all daisies (I say almost merely to protect myself) the calyx is formed of sepals overlapping each other like fish scales. When the florets have ripened and the seeds are dispersed the shell remains and usually persists on the old stems until these disintegrate. Many of these sepals, for example those of thistles, are lined with a silvery skin which gives them a moonlight quality. Even the dowdy groundsel weed bears stems of little stars after the fluffy seeds have gone. (See plate p71.)

Do seek them out for yourself. Often the plant needs a little prompting from you before it reveals its possession. For example, the stars of some of the species of centaurea often to be found on sale in natural form and bleached, still retain the old tuft of faded petals. So too do any of this tribe found growing wild. If these are cleaned by removing all traces of the old flower you can then see how decorative is the structure which held them. If you are patient and slowly but firmly open these calyces you can make open 'stars' of them.

In some cases the fluffy cluster of old florets is left in some dried materials you buy: artichokes and cardoons, for instance. Sometimes this is dyed.

Thistles of all kinds may not be pleasant to gather but many of them are really very beautiful. Wire these while they are still supple if you can. It will make things much easier later on.

*CLEMATIS VITALBA*, traveller's joy or old man's beard and other species which have handsome fluffy seed heads should be preserved in glycerine and water otherwise they will gradually disintegrate. If they are treated properly they will last for years.

The best time to gather the stems is the moment that the flower petals drop. There is no evidence at this point that these will become fluffy, judging by a casual glance.

Pick long stems of vitalba, retaining the foliage. Only cut this away where it is damaged in some way.

Before putting the stem ends in the hot glycerine solution, first split them upwards for an inch or two then stand them for a while in water which is at boiling point. Take them out before this cools and put them immediately in the hot solution.

If you want only short stems, or if you are treating some of the other species which grow differently, treat them in exactly the same way but keep the fluffy styles out of both water and solution.

*CROCOSMIA CROCOSMAEFLORA*, montbretia, which grows in so many gardens offers a seed stem with a different shape from many others. These should be cut soon after the flowers have faded although any which have faded naturally on the plant are usually quite good to use.

When gathered green they can either be given the glycerine treatment, or they can be dried by method 1. The long leaves can be left on the stem and will dry quite well. They are sometimes improved in appearance by being ironed.

*DIPSACUS SYLVESTRIS*, teasel. Teasels, great favourites of mine, have the charm of being very long stemmed. Many tall materials often look unbalanced when placed high in an arrangement with shorter materials below, but though these perpetuelles are fairly large they are not dense or heavy. Furthermore, the stems are much-branching with smaller heads round the larger terminal heads so that it is always possible to cut some smaller specimens from a stem. Where necessary, the stems can be cut quite short for arrangement without detriment to the look of the teasel itself. (See plate p36.)

Florists sell dyed teasels and readers have written to tell me that they have successfully dyed them with domestic dyes.

*D. fullonum*, the fuller's teasel, is similar to sylvestris but its bracts are more hooked. *D. laciniatus* is more erect with the bracts, which make a collar round the base of the head, somewhat shorter than they are in the other species.

*FRITILLARIA MELEAGRIS*, the little chequered lily or fritillary, hangs its head in life but as the seeds ripen, the stems grow erect until at last the little wooden lily-shaped 'flower' is cupped to the sky. If you are lucky enough to have other fritillarias watch for their seed cases too. They are almost certain to be lovely. Let the seed ripen before you gather them.

GLADIOLI. The species and varieties can be treated in the same way. It may not be good gardening to let these go to seed (the corm benefits if the flower spike is removed as soon as the florets fade) but the ripe brown seed stems look well in 'wooden' and other ensembles.

IRISES, like the plants in the lily tribe and other nearly related families, yield good seed pods, some, such as the *I. foetidissima*, being filled with shining red or orange berries. Unfortunately, once the berries are ripe they easily fall from the pods. To prevent this, as soon as the iris is gathered, or as soon as possible after, the surface of the berries should be sprayed or brushed (the first is best) with a colourless adhesive.

The *I. sibirica* and others leave behind them some neat seed vessels, several to one tall stem. These should be left to become quite ripe and they can be used right away.

If you grow irises of any kind, or you know where some grow, keep watch on them as they fade. They may produce some very useful materials for you.

LABIATES are a good source of interesting seed stems for many of the flowers have calyces which dry well, most of them set in whorls about the stem which gives the spike an attractive shape. One of the loveliest of them is specially grown for these calyces. This is *Moluccella laevis*, the shell flower, sometimes called bells of Ireland. Its good strong stems are studded with limpet-shaped calyces each surrounding a tiny white-lipped flower. These stems dry well but they do not retain their colour. They usually dry a light tan or a silvery beige.

All garden labiates are worth examining after they have flowered. Sages, of which there are many, have some attractive plants among them. *Phlomis fruticosa*, the Jerusalem sage, a grey-leaved shrub, has globular heads of grey-green calyces remaining after the yellow flowers have gone.

*LEONOTIS LEONURUS* a South African species, has long stems handsomely decorated with whorls of calyces. These are often on sale in florists.

*LUNARIA ANNUA*, honesty, is one of the loveliest and certainly one of the most abused of dried materials! The portion of the plant so esteemed is not the seed pod but only part of it, the dividing wall or placenta between the two seed chambers. When the seed pods are dried and mature enough it is possible to strip away these two outer layers quite easily. This happens quite naturally when the pods are left on the plant but by that time the tissues have become so brittle that they have also become damaged. The 'moons' are also soiled to some degree.

It is important that honesty should look as bright as possible. For this reason the seed stems should not be left to mature on the plant but should be gathered as soon as they are a good size. Wait until the seed is well formed and can be seen inside the case. As a rule, at this stage, the pods are changing in hue from their original colour. Stems may then be cut and hung upside down until they are dry. Alternatively, pull the plant up by the root and hang.

Young green and green-purple unstripped pods can be dried and used entire for some arrangements. These can also be given glycerine when you will get interesting results!

*NIGELLA DAMASCENA*, love-in-a-mist, leaves behind enchanting pepper-pot shaped seed boxes still decorated with fern-like bracts below them. The sooner you gather these the better chance you have of keeping them a good colour but then you may have to sacrifice size for hue. However, the pleasant tan of the dried seed heads is quite attractive and it blends in well with almost all other perpetuelles.

I like to pull up the entire plant by its root and let it dry slowly. Sometimes when I do this, tiny, newly opened flowers dry and remain the lovely blue.

OKRA, *Hibiscus esculentus*, leaves behind it long pointed seed cases, remains of the 'lady-fingers' vegetable which are the seed pods when green. There are usually three pods to a stem, but they can, of course, be detached and used individually.

SAPONARIA seed heads of various species are readily available. Many of these are garden plants, others grow wild in most countries. Those on sale are usually bleached and I find that the stems are stiff and the branches close

81

together. These can be induced to return to their natural manner by patiently pulling the side stems away from the centre stem. The stems often have to be pruned considerably if they are to give a graceful effect but all the trimmings can be used in smaller arrangements.

These are members of the carnation family and in passing I would like to point out that even the seed cases of bought carnations can be kept and dried. Simply pull the faded petals from them and then dry them quickly by method 2.

**SPIRAEAS, ASTILBES** and **FILIPENDULA** are all nearly related. Many of them are garden plants. They should be gathered while they are 'new' and before rain, frost and weather generally has made them shabby. Some of them are in fine, warm russet-browns. The astilbes generally have attractive spicate shapes.

Obviously, there must be many more seed heads than those I have mentioned here. Obviously too, we do not all see things through the same eyes and what may seem lovely to me may repel someone else. I have described those I know and have handled. I would like to feel that I have stimulated the uninitiated to go out and begin the search! There is a rich reward. One never knows how beautifully plants are designed until one sees the bare fabric. Fortunately for the arranger, these same skeletons have no hint of cruel death, only the soft pleasant peace of a sleeping winter time.

CHAPTER 7

# Nuts, fruits and cones

You may be surprised to see fruits included in a book on dried flowers but only a few that I mention are the succulent kinds; the others are fruits in the botanical sense. Even so, the succulent kinds are there for a special reason. I like to use them—and they include those which are known as 'vegetables'—to bring a fresh and lively note to perpetuelles. Not all are short lived. Some of them, gourds for instance, will last a year, but others are much more fleeting.

Even so, they have their uses. A semi-permanent dried arrangement can be changed quite frequently in a matter of minutes simply by planning that it should have a living focal point of fresh materials, either all of one kind or a mixture. But more of this in Chapter 11.

## Berries

Berries abound in many countries. Few of them will last for more than a few weeks when cut, depending on their surroundings and whether or not they are in water. It is possible to keep them plump a little longer by spraying them with lacquer to keep the air in. Others can be given a

83

short dose of glycerine solution twenty-four hours or so before being either put back in water or else arranged and left to dry. It really is a matter of experimenting.

Some berries will dry in a sense, and remain effective for some weeks. The symphoricarpos or snowberry is one of these and I find the fine arching sprays of pendulous berry clusters very useful for arranging low in groups, especially in ensembles of grey and white perpetuelles. Alternatively, one can use fresh stems and keep them in water, changing them with fresh supplies when necessary.

Pernettya, privet, iris, callicarpa, berberis and some rose hips are all kinds I have used and allowed to dry and which have remained effective for a good long period. Florist sundriesmen sell dried bayberries, *Myrica californica*, and sometimes also *M. cerifera*. The fruits, which are studded close to the stems, are covered with a wax-like resin. Other myricas can be used and are worth growing or collecting.

*PHYSALIS ALKEKENGI* has berries which very cleverly provide covers for themselves. Together they make the so-called Chinese lantern or winter cherry. The Cape gooseberry is the edible version and its lanterns are nothing like so handsomely coloured, although its fruits are delicious! It is a lovely thing, quite the brightest of our perpetuelles. It is also an easily grown perennial. Unlike the uncovered berries it lasts a long time.

The attractive sprays of fruits should be gathered just as soon as the first lantern turns orange but before the frosts and damp of autumn have spoiled their colours and textures. The green lanterns will soon turn colour as they dry. Remove the leaves from the stems and the tip also but do this neatly so that there is no ugly stem projecting beyond the topmost lantern.

The stems can be arranged immediately for they will dry

in situ. Otherwise they may be dried by method 1. Should any lanterns become squashed and mis-shapen during harvesting you can restore them to their former plumpness by blowing through the tiny aperture at the point at the base. (See plates p53.)

Physalis looks particularly well in wall vases and other hanging decorations where a great part of the materials need to be pendant. If it is intended to use the stems this way, or if they are to be arranged low in large standing arrangements, obviously any natural curve of a stem will aid the arranger. One can exploit the slightest curve by inserting a strong wire—or more should the stem be thick and heavy—inside the base of the stem while it is still moist.

Alternatively, splice the stem and the wires or use fine canes if wires are not available. Thus the wire or the cane which is to go down inside the container will be absolutely straight and bare while all the curved decorative portion is displayed. The stem can be bent at the place where wire is inserted and thus the lanterned portion can be made really pendant where this is desirable.

Sometimes some stems are not well furnished and there may be only one or two lanterns remaining. Such stems can be divided into sections and used as one would use any single stemmed bloom. Alternatively, a number of lanterns can be mounted individually on fine wires and then arranged on a long stem or covered wire using much the same method as that employed in making spikes of flowers which is explained in the chapter on Assembly, page 122. Assembled this way also, opened lanterns can be made into sprays of flowers (see page 146).

I like to use the individual lanterns also in Byzantine cones, sometimes using these alone simply interspersed with snippets of evergreen, sometimes mixing them with a variety of other 'fruits'.

*NICANDRA PHYSALOIDES* is another plant which behaves in so similar a manner that it has been named after the physalis. This is also called the shoo-fly plant because it is supposed to be unattractive to these insects. The lanterns on the nicandra are firmer than those on the other plant and they are not so brightly coloured. They dry a greenish-tan, very light in tint, but they are attractive and, being an annual of Peru, easily grown.

If you have the patience, you can skeletonise these in the same way as leaves. To clean the lanterns of the dead tissues use a nylon washing-up brush and treat them gently.

CAPSICUMS and PEPPERS of all kinds can be used to liven up a dried arrangement. Handled carefully and mounted on false stems without damaging the fruits, these waxy yellow, scarlet or green, rounded, pointed, gnome-like fruits will add a great splash of gleaming colour in vase or swag arrangements. They are particularly useful for the latter.

GOURDS are grown in the same way as marrows, pumpkins and squash. There are many varieties and their colours range through orange, white, green and yellow and they are round, egg-shaped, pear-shaped or bottle-necked. Some are plain coloured, some striped, some smooth, others covered with carbuncles. All of them are lovely.

To keep them successfully for months on end they should be handled with great care after they are gathered even though the skin feels wood hard. Treat them like eggs. When you gather them do not pile them one on the other but keep them well apart to allow them to dry out and harden further.

They should not be gathered until they are quite ripe otherwise they will become soft or mouldy. Rap on them!

If the skins are hard they can be cut. Try to cut as much of the little stem as possible. This is not always retained by the ripe fruit but when it is, mounting on false stems is much easier, as you can imagine. If you intend to mount some gourds on false stems or wires, which have to be inserted, be prepared for them not to last as long as the others.

## Tree seeds

These are legion and the cases which hold them are often both beautiful and useful to the flower arranger. Florists' sundriesmen and specialists in perpetuelles sell an ever increasing variety of them with names like camphor pods, lipstick pods, acacia, bell eucalyptus, coral tree beans, wili-wili and woodroses, to mention only a few.

Meanwhile, all around us and in every country, there are plenty to be found. Hornbeam (carpinus), beech (fagus), maple (acer), oak (quercus) and many others are worth saving. If the branches are gathered before the end of the season and given glycerine treatment they will retain their seed cases as well as their leaves.

Often the keys of maple and sycamore are beautifully coloured when they are young. If they are gathered then and dried by method 1 they will retain much of their colour, although they will become more and more tan as they age. They will retain enough of the rose and pink to pick up any hint of the hue in any companion materials which may be arranged with the keys, so that the hint of colour becomes enhanced and of greater value.

The round tassels of the London plane and the American buttonwoods picked before they are quite mature can be induced to hang gracefully from wall decorations or over the rim of some standing container.

Often the area under trees is rich with the fallen seeds

and seed cases. Beech nut carpels, like little four-petalled wooden flowers, beautifully cupped acorns, winged keys and others should be gathered and stored ready to be transformed into flowers or to be used either alone or in small bunches in swags, garlands and cones, all described in Chapter 10.

The thick-textured, conical, pitted fruits of the magnolia can be used for their own sakes alone when they will have to be mounted on false stems. But they are also extremely effective when used as centres for any 'flowers' you may make. You can for instance make a 'magnolia' by using skeletonised (shadow) magnolia leaves as 'petals'. Each of these will have to be mounted on thin wire and grouped round the seed head, also mounted but on a stronger wire. The flowers can be single or double. If you cared to carry this further, these same flowers could be accompanied by sprays of preserved magnolia leaves mounted on bare branches so that they looked as life-like as possible (see Chapter 10).

Florist sundriesmen sell these seed heads, usually in their natural state. I find that they suit grey and 'silver' foliage well and another way I use them is to mount them in the centre of a rosette of mullein, or verbascum.

If you wish to retain such nuts as hazel and acorns in their original state, complete with cup, gather them before they become quite ripe and let them dry. Alternatively, use a little adhesive and fix the nut to the cup as soon as it is gathered. If it is ripe it will leave its cup quite easily and replacing it is only a matter of moments but worth doing.

My favourite materials and certainly those for which I find most use are cones, little wooden flowers, agreeable, ready to mix with almost every other perpetuelle which comes their way. And they are so varied! They range from the tiny clusters on thuja and cupressus to the great pine

*Page 89* Straws threaded through the lowest lying flowers helps them to hang gracefully and gives the arrangement a more natural appearance than if the blooms were wired. The thistles and foliage are Australian (p128)

*(right)* Sprigs of holly were arranged fresh and allowed to dry in this arrangement. Other perpetuelles include eucalyptus, phlomis seed heads, gourds and araucaria 'flower' (p58)

*(below)* analogous colour harmony, yellow, orange and red helichrysums, yellow achillea, orange 'berries' of *Iris foetidissima* or gladwin iris, in gilded basket on a copper stand (p8)

cones. Some of the long cones can be cut into sections to make wooden flowers which are somewhat zinnia-like in appearance.

Although so many people use cones at Christmas time when they are 'frosted' with sparkle and paint or enamelled various bright colours, few consider using them for the rest of the year. Most mixed groups of dried materials are improved by the addition of cones although, naturally, the type of cone used is important.

Larch cones come ready mounted and prettily arranged on stems, which curve and taper most obligingly. They need little aid from us. It is best to shave or clean with a knife the lower portion of stem to make them smooth so that they may be arranged quickly and easily.

The branches which you find under trees are usually the old growths. The cones on them are darker than those on the tree itself but they are not spoiled with age. All cones are very long lasting. As with most things, variety in the hues and shades brings a lovelier and more satisfying effect to the finished design so, if you can, gather some of the current year's branches from the tree. In some areas the larch trees become heavily festooned with lichen and are often very lovely. I have more to say about this in the following chapter.

Larch branches may need some pruning or grooming. Keep any coneless side stems for these come in useful for holding other wooden fruits and items such as nuts, beech mast, chestnuts and even some real flowers and leaves.

Cones will need no special treatment to preserve them. Sometimes, when they are gathered in wet weather or perhaps from wet ground, they may be both muddy and closed tight. They should then be washed in warm soapy water and laid out in some warm dry place to open.

The tiny cones on thuja and cupressus and similar conifers can be gathered with the foliage. This usually dries quite well and remain intact for about a year.

Highly decorative and on a very small scale individually are the tiny wooden cases of the alder. These are black and resemble tiny cones but they are in little bunches or sprays. The branches themselves are attractively gnarled and most decorative.

Some plants produce berry-like capsules, some hypericums or St John's wort, are examples. In most cases, these begin by looking lush and berry-like and may be green, yellow, orange and red. Ultimately, the texture hardens and the berries darken. They become dry and hard to the touch. This is the point at which they should be gathered. Remove the leaves and simply hang the stems up to finish drying. They can also be arranged right away.

*Hypericum androsaemum* has dark brown berry-like capsule clusters which can be gathered on long stems. The main cluster is flanked by smaller ones and I find it best to remove these. They can be mounted on false stems and used elsewhere. These heads offer a different shape from most other perpetuelles. I find them useful also as 'fillers' and 'fabric' for Byzantine cones, for grouping in garlands and as a background for cones and other wooden fruits.

From time to time I have referred to 'wooden' materials; this seems to me to be the most apt and descriptive way of classifying them. Cones and nuts are good examples and there are many more which cry out to be used in what I sometimes call 'treen' arrangements.

The lovely deeply pitted seed heads of the lotus, magnolia, camphor, eucalyptus, monk bread tree, woodroses, and many other unfamiliar materials are just some of those an arranger can hope to buy.

Each country has its own botanical treasures. The arranger may see and admire them yet be reluctant to harvest them because it is sometimes difficult to see how they could be arranged or used. In my experience, it is only the very large items or sometimes those which are either very long or extremely convoluted that present real problems. Anything which is the size of any flower one is likely to use in a fresh arrangement usually can be mounted, even if it has no stem, and be used like a flower.

# CHAPTER 8

# Bark, branch, lichen and fungus

To the perceptive flower arranger all parts of a plant are considered as of the same value as a bloom. The term 'flower' is an umbrella which covers all. Bark and branch, root and stem, so long as they have some claim to beauty and purpose, can be regarded as an integral part of an arrangement.

And in the same way, those plants which do not produce blooms, the fungi, lichens and mosses, are also considered as part of the great resources of plant material at the decorator's disposal.

As with all the other perpetuelles described so far, the importer and merchant can offer bark, branch, root, lichen and fungus and these include long graceful stems of embryo dates, dried embryo palm leaf and others, manzanita stems, chollo wood, slices of yucca stem, palmetto flower, dried bracket fungus, tundra or Iceland moss, driftwood and eucalyptus among many others. Some of these are used in arrangements, some to frame them, some like the yucca stem and cocoa boats to hold them.

It is possible to buy little containers made of certain

barks in which flowers can be displayed, but you can also make your own. Some trees provide better bark than others. The cork oak is perhaps the most useful of all. It is cleaned and free from pests when it is bought from the florist sundriesman.

The silver birches will yield a soft and silky bark which is more pliable than most. Silver birch containers are often sold in nests of three different sizes. These are useful for small arrangements. They consist of a circular base to which the strip of bark is attached. (See plate p54.)

Often where trees have been felled you can find good strips of bark. There are almost always bound to be insects under bark though these, as a rule, disappear quite quickly once they are disturbed. When you arrive home leave the bark in the sun and also in a place where birds can get at it in case there are insects you have overlooked. When it is dry brush it well inside and out with a soft brush.

To use bark either as a cover for, or even as a complete container, it is quite simple to mould it to the size and pattern required. For a tin or jar to be camouflaged, select a strip or piece long and wide enough to cover it. It is best not to make the edge of the rim too precise but to let the outline be a little rugged and if possible a little higher in some parts than others. The lower edge should be quite straight. Alternatively, raise it just a fraction of an inch from the base of the hidden inner container so that it stands firm.

Lay the bark in water (salted to kill any lurking insects) for a few hours or until the bark is pliable. When you wrap it round the container, strong elastic bands will hold it in place. If you intend to make a container of bark alone, use a vessel as a mould. Leave the bands in place until the bark has hardened and curled.

Bark containers can be filled with plastic bags to prevent

any 'crumbs' of the stem-holder escaping.

A log of wood, particularly those kinds with silky and attractive bark such as birch, hazel, arbutus or bamboo, can be scooped out to make containers. These can be either laid on their sides or used upright. As you probably know, thick sections of bamboo look well treated this way.

Slices of wood, usually first polished or veneered, can be scooped out in one area so that one can sink a small container. Alternatively, a container can be screwed to its surface. Yet another way is to fix a log to the wood slice.

Branches of many trees and shrubs can be used in perpetuelle arrangements both bare or holding either leaves, seeds or lichen. Where a good deal of wall space is to be covered by the decoration, branches are often most useful. Sometimes they can be used solely for the sake of their form and colour. Alder, complete with tiny cones and dried catkins, is one I like to show in silhouette. Some branches have brightly coloured bark and a good outline. *Cornus stolonifera*, the red osier dogwood is one of these. Its stems are a lovely rich wine-red. True osiers or willows yield orange and chrome stems and keep their colours after drying.

In the chapter dealing with foliage I described some of the branches which can be dried or otherwise preserved and I would like to expand on this theme a little. Quite often one needs to do no more than gather the branch, trim it if necessary and arrange it where it is to stand. It can then either make a decoration in its own right or it can serve as the fabric for an arrangement later to be embroidered with other perpetuelles.

For this purpose you can gather stems of the evergreen *Garrya elliptica* whose long silver catkins are produced during November to February. The branches can be gathered at any time after the catkins appear but, naturally, if you wait until these are elongated you will have a more decorative branch.

Almost all branches bearing catkins, whether evergreen or bare, can be treated this way. In cases where the long lamb's tail type of catkins, hazel for instance, are used, cut the branch while the catkins are just at their best. They will then dry and keep yellow. In time they become brittle but if they are left undisturbed as much as possible, they will last for months.

There are various ways in which the pretty pussy willows, *Salix caprea, discolor, daphnoides* and other species can be used in dried flower arrangements. As with those I have just described, the branches can be cut—this time before the catkins are fully opened and covered with pollen—and arranged right away.

Alternatively, the stems can be hung until required. The dried stems can later be divided to provide short lengths, each holding a few catkins. It is possible too, for small arrangements, to mount individual catkins on wires and use them as though they were tiny blooms.

Certain distorted forms of willow have their uses. Good curves can be given to straight stems by bending the branches into hoops, tying them in one or two places to keep them in shape and soaking them for several hours in water. Usually, these hoops have to be weighted down. Branches with catkins on should not be left in water or they lose them. Instead, tie the branches into hoops or some other required shape, for instance an S-bend, and leave them to dry.

An easy and effective way of inducing unusual curves is to tie the branches in the required shapes though somewhat more exaggerated than necessary, while they are still on the tree. Let them remain growing until they are required for arrangement some time later. With a few branches curved in this way, very simple yet lovely designs can be carried out. For example, in a pewter tankard willow branches, gleaming with the catkins, curving away from the handle in lovely arcs may frame a round mop of dried blue-green hydrangea backed by a silver-leaved rosette of mullein.

In winter, budded branches placed in water can frame a low arrangement of dried materials. This gives a pleasant age-and-youth type of composition. It is a simple matter to arrange the fresh branches so that they can be removed and replaced when necessary.

Like the fasciated willow I mentioned earlier, there are some plants which are naturally contorted. One of these is a hazel, *Corylus avellana contorta*. Branches cut before the buds open can be dried successfully and so, as you might expect, can those which bear catkins.

Ivy, both the branches of the adult or 'tree' form and the netted 'root-wood', which can be found both on trees and walls, often grows in an interesting fashion providing good 'line' material for the decorator. Sometimes, especially on sunbaked walls, one can find extremely attractive pieces already stripped by the weather and bleached by the sun. On the other hand, those pieces still covered with bark can be soaked and later stripped when they peel easily when tested.

On heaths and moorlands you·can often find twisted and well-branched pieces of stems and roots of gorse. The first have been stripped of their spines by fire and washed clean of soot by rain. In the same terrain sometimes whole skeletons of heather plants can be found. Both gorse and heath may have to be divided into less fussy pieces before they can be arranged properly.

Most treasured of all branches by flower arrangers is driftwood, found most plentifully on shores near the mouths of rivers and streams or along the rivers themselves. Sometimes you can find it on the shores of lakes. Driftwood looks well with dried materials of all kinds and it can be found in sufficient variety to provide sturdy pieces for large items and daintier forms for the smaller perpetuelles. Quite often flat pieces can be used as a base and the arrangement fixed directly on it in some form of stem holder. A combination of a wood base and driftwood 'frame' for a mixture of preserved leaves and 'wooden' perpetuelles can be very lovely and extremely pleasing to the eye.

A real windfall that once came my way was a branch of araucaria, the monkey-puzzle tree. Part of the brown branch (for the leaves were 'dead'), the most pliable portion, was simply curved to make a Christmas garland. The remainder was cut into sections and became a useful collection of 'cone' flowers.

Earlier, I said that larch branches festooned with lichen were very lovely. So are any others which become so decorated. Many trees and shrubs which grow in damp situations are often covered or festooned with hoary grey-green lichen and although this does not keep its soft sponge-like character once it is arranged in a dry warm room, it does keep its shape and what can only be described as its personality.

Fortunately, lichen is a good mixer. Rose, pink, white, orange, yellow and red immortelles blend with its soft neutral hues and texture as well as the soft colours of bark and branch and all the muted tones of the 'wooden' subjects.

From time to time, I detach large pieces of lichen from stems, usually from the ends which have to be stripped anyway, and wire or otherwise mount them to use in an arrangement. Pieces that become detached can be fixed to fine larch stems with adhesive. I often use pieces of flat lichen in plaques and pictures. It does not, as a rule, need pressing first.

If the lichen branches are to be arranged and stood in a very hot, dry atmosphere they should be sprayed lightly with a clear thin laquer to prevent them from dropping quickly.

One lovely lichen which does not grow on trees but beneath them is the beautiful silvery grey lichen moss, tundra or Iceland moss. This is used a great deal in European floristry. Sometimes whole funeral wreaths and other designs are made from it. The experimenting arranger will find that it is willing to hobnob with almost every kind of plant material. It is useful as a 'filler' and used at rim level or just above so that other stems can rise from it. It can also be mounted and used in swags, garlands and as a foundation fabric on cones.

The lichen is usually bought from the florist or florist sundriesman. Before using, it is best soaked when it will become sponge-like and pliable. It should be cleaned when wet as it is then easier to remove the dross, mainly pine needles, embedded in it.

Many fungi may be dried and used in a number of ways. Some dry quite naturally and easily and with no special treatment. Bracket fungus, the oyster fungus growing on tree trunks is a good example. Others can be dried by method 2 and by dessicants. (See plate p72.)

Some are attractive whether used the right way up or with the underside uppermost. Those of the bracket fungi group, ganoderma, are examples. The tops are often beautifully crusted while the undersides show an interesting pattern of gills. Little clusters can be prised off tree trunks where some will be found already dried which means that you can find a variation in tones.

Some of the larger tree fungi are often bowl shaped and after drying can be used as containers. These can be fixed to a plaque made of tree bark and the perpetuelles arranged inside them.

Some of the cup-shaped fungi, cantharellus and clitocybe,

can be dried and then transformed into 'flowers'. A grass straw can be threaded down through the centre. These make attractive little items and give the arranger an extra shape to play with.

I find fungi surprisingly useful in all kinds of arrangements and I have no compunction about using the large types in fresh flower arrangements where they cover pinholders effectively at the same time as they are part of the design. For dried flowers, I like to place them at the foot of a 'tree' of some branch or a piece of driftwood and blend them with the rugged and wooden materials rather than with everlastings.

Some of the variety of dried materials sold by the sundriesmen are from less obvious parts of plants and perhaps a description of them will serve to show just how much material might be near at hand. For instance, desert pine is the young tip of a conifer. Others of this family also have tips and these can be dried if you think that they are likely to fit in with the style of arrangements you plan to make.

Coconut spathe and cocoa-boats are the brown woody structures which are so tough in texture that they can be used as containers for certain styles of arrangements.

The so-called areca boots are the stems with swollen bases from the palm of that name. Desert spoons are the stem ends of agave and yuccas.

In some cases the whole skeleton of a plant may be sold, for instance, the so-called desert primrose which is a cactus. Some pot-grown cacti, past their best, might be more decorative if skeletonised and used in an arrangement.

Embryo palm shoots and leaves, still tightly curled, are dried and sold. These are most effective in contemporary and line designs.

So-called palm plumes, florettes, blossom, calyx and strands are the inflorescences of various species of palms.

**101**

Among the roots which have decorative value and which are also sold are vine-roots, twisted and gnarled, heavier rosemary and smilax, twisted cypress. The former are often sand-blasted to make them look like driftwood.

All flower arrangers will know the value of pieces of beautifully shaped driftwood and these can be used in perpetuelle decorations as well as fresh flower arrangements. Branches of similar form and for similar use as driftwood include ghost-wood or manzanita, and gum branches, which are more finely branched. These are on sale.

Cholla is the skeleton stem of a tree cactus.

# CHAPTER 9

# Colour and design

Most of the natural dried materials have broken colours.
Exceptions are a few everlastings or immortelles, but you
are unlikely to see much scarlet, bright blue, yellow, orange
or lively green in the drained skeletons of plant life. Indeed,
the broken colours, the tans, beiges, browns, olives, greys
and duns are the dried materials themselves, just ghosts of
something once bright and living, full of light, the source
of colour.

But even ghosts charm some people and intrigue most of
us! There is an ever growing army of enthusiasts for the
dried arrangement. Indeed, once converted, the flower arranger finds them indispensable for certain occasions or
settings.

Naturally the enthusiasts fall into two schools. In one we
find the purists, the arrangers who love the dried things for
their own beauty, for their own soft muted colours. Such
people disdain to use any dyed materials but will accept
those leaves that have been artificially preserved even
though their original colour is lost. In the other school we
have those to whom all plant material is grist to the mill.
Some people, the florists for example, have no choice, for

customers have many tastes and all these tastes have to be catered for.

Although I lean more to the 'natural materials only' school I really belong to both and it is really only natural that I should. At one time I deplored all dyed materials and often had some biting things to say about them. But living as I do when in town, in the middle of the world's largest flower market, I have been forced to observe that the other half of the world likes its dried flowers not only dyed but coloured as brightly as could be, 'shudderingly bright' as a young friend described it. They also like them bleached almost white rather than lightened in tone.

When I first became interested in dried flower arrangement most of these garish materials were so often set into the badly designed 'bird's nest' type of arrangement that there seemed, at that time, to be nothing one could do about it. When an offer came to me to act as consultant to a firm that specialised in these materials I accepted gladly and for some years I conducted a modest campaign for more harmonious colour schemes. I was able to do this to a great degree through the various trade papers for which I wrote. It was not long before I received my reward. One evening driving along a part of London where little floral colour finds its way, I saw in a florist's shop window a display of replicas of my own designs and colour schemes. The sincerest form of flattery!

At the other end of the scale, an arrangement of naturally coloured perpetuelles I made for a friend's contemporary flat brought the observation, 'Well, do you know I never liked those things before. And what lovely colours! I always thought that everlastings were purple and that dull bronze.' These were glowing yellow helichrysums, gnaphaliums, pale erianthus, white helichrysums, vivid orange physalis and yellow bracken.

Nowadays I do not hesitate to mix all kinds together according to the function of the decoration, for there is a fitness to be observed in all things. But one must have a rule to guide one; a star, or in this case, a spectrum, to steer by.

The situation as I see it is this. Those who love the dried materials for their own sakes have no colour problems. The hues on their palettes are all broken colours, or mostly all. The materials they use are the skeletons, the sketches and etchings of plant life, and they draw them in dark, mid- and light-brown, biscuit, beige and tan, dark, light and blue-grey, olive and truly a thousand other colours with just an occasional hint of orange or some other pure colour. The important thing is that all these broken hues are modest. None are dominating. It is possible to mix them all together and create pleasant quiet harmonies sung in an undertone, as it were, with no loud discordant clashes.

Like the colours at their disposal the materials for the purists are also limitless. Obviously the plantsman has the best of the bargain for such materials are not accessible to all. But there is a greater rub, as I have already hinted. Not all want them. The unsophisticated artists are legion. They do not appreciate the beauties of the drained plant structure. Give them a seed pod and they will paint it white and stipple it with blue.

However, because so large a proportion of the public has demanded more and more perpetuelle materials in more colours and hues their demands have been met and the experimental among us are faced with a choice. Shall we say 'only natural materials' or shall we say—must we say—'I like some of the dyed materials but I am not sure if I should use them!' There are others among us who say, 'I am sure I could make pretty arrangements even with these vulgar colours'. Others want to 'know how' simply in order to earn a living. Perhaps my experience will help the wavering to make a choice.

In the first place it is worth considering that all dried materials, whether dyed or natural, have something in common—their texture. Arrange soft fresh yellow daisies with fresh lily-of-the-valley and they will not look incongruous but take the fresh daisies away and replace them with yellow helichrysum and you will soon see that something is wrong. This quality of texture helps us over our first hurdle for we know that our materials have an affinity, each is *en rapport* with the other. But more than that is needed to make a pleasing arrangement of mixed perpetuelles.

One of the fundamentals of a successful flower arrangement of any kind is a suitable container and I believe that for perpetuelle arrangements in particular this is the most important item of all. It seems hardly possible to-day that dried flowers were once to be seen arranged in cut glass or that at one time gilt baskets were considered the receptacle for 'winter' bouquets. In this direction the flower clubs have helped more than we can truly estimate. By showing their members that natural wood bark is the ideal medium for fungi, grasses and foliage, to take just one example, they have caused many a person to stop and think and, finally, to make another and more suitable choice. The important things a container should contribute to an arrangement or a composition are suitability, colour and texture.

Strangely enough although white is so constantly used for fresh flowers it was not until recent years that it came to be used as a container colour in conjunction with perpetuelles.

White is a colour which should never be overlooked by the arranger, especially if the arrangements are being designed for sale. It imparts a summer freshness to dried blooms. Where possible one should include a little white in

*Page 107 (left)* In a swag, mixed cones are best graded or grouped. Here larch cones are at the tip and are also introduced from time to time among the larch cones. Swags can be kept from year to year and trimmed afresh with new evergreens (p137); *(above)* made on a wire frame, a garland of pine and larch cones, sweet chestnut burrs, beech mast, acorns, lupin seed pods, *Hypericum androssaemum* berries, yew, holly and thuja foliage (p137)

*(right)* Two cycas palm fronds, painted and glittered, curved and fastened to a wire hoop to make a door garland for Christmas, with pine, thuja, holly and red bell baubles (p55)

*(below)* 'Christmas roses' made from honesty moons and gold threaded ribbon grouped with gilded holly leaves for a gift wrap decoration. The 'roses' can also be mounted and used in other forms of decoration

the ingredients of the arrangement to link the one with the other and also to catch and reflect the slightest amount of light. In an odd sort of way, white containers 'clean' dried flowers whereas a dull one will not only absorb them but give them a damning anonymity.

I have more to say about containers in Chapter 11. Meanwhile, back to the dyed materials.

To understand their colour possibilities one has to realise that here we are faced with a new problem for the flower arranger who has always dealt in fresh flowers. We have all the spectrum colours, red, yellow-red, yellow, green-yellow, green, green-blue, blue, purple-blue, purple and red-purple, without the infusion of green which is almost always present in fresh flowers and which acts as a buffer or softener to dominant colours.

This is one reason, perhaps an unconscious one, why so many people dislike dyed plant materials. But it makes our task of colour blending fairly simple. Natural contrasts may be used but we have to supply the link that lifts them from mixtures of blocks of colour to beautifully harmonised flower arrangements.

Take, for example, violet and yellow dyed gnaphalium, natural complementary colours. Arranged together in, say a gilt basket, whether the heads are used formally or re-assembled in spikes or sprays, I do not think that the arranger would contribute much to the world of floral art. But the arranger who knows, grows or collects plant materials has a great advantage. Given the colour start of the two bright yet natural colour complementaries—even though the materials are dyed—the theme is set. All one needs to do is to add to the dyed violet some softer, natural violet, shall be say, eryngium, *Limonium latifolium*, a touch of *L. sinuata* and some catananche, and to the yellow, brighter yellow helichrysums, softer 'smudged' yellow fronds of soli-

109

dago, the drained yellow of barley or perhaps rye-grass, and a few light tan beech leaves which are a tint of the broken colour which is made by combining violet with yellow.

By doing this we surround the dyed flowers with a frame, a buffer, of natural hues. They lose a little of their identity. As the strident colours become merged with the others, each takes on a little of the other's individuality. In fact, they harmonise.

Sometimes, some of the dyed colours seem too unreal to be associated with flowers and yet careful blending will veil that unreality. The proportion of colour used is important. Always use more natural material than dyed and try to surround the dyed colour with the nearest to it in the natural you have, placing the deepest and tones nearest to it in colour, closest to it. Graduate these out to the tints or to those materials that have only a hint of the basic colour. If you have no harmonising materials of this kind use greens or the nearest thing to green that you can find among the natural perpetuelles.

When you are using two colours the broken colours made by mixing them together will supply a restraining touch. Let me explain what broken colours are. Next time you get close to a grey pigeon in the street or in the woods, stand a while and note the colours in its plumage. Round its neck you will see the red-purple, the magenta which I am discussing, and mingled with this will be the lovely spectrum green. If these two colours were paints and we blended them together the result would be the grey of the pigeon's plumage. Odd perhaps, but true. The grey is the colour made by breaking the two spectrum colours.

From this perhaps you can see why it is that the grey of lichen moss (a tint of dove grey), pussy willow, lamb's ear and senecio look so lovely and are so pleasing when seen with natural magenta helichrysums and why the little touch of brightly dyed green grasses is not so offensive as one might expect it to be.

These three, the two colours and the broken colour, belong to each other and because they belong they will always look right. We can take this a little further and say that their tints, shades and tones will also look right. Which means that a tint of magenta so pale that it is almost white, and green so dark that it is almost black, as well as the deeper pinks and the paler greens will all harmonise attractively. Some people know without any kind of technical training that these colours blend together and are 'right'. Others have to learn either by trial and error or by playing with a box of paints.

My advice then for brilliantly dyed materials, no matter what they are, is to select the spectrum colours, where possible to use the natural complementaries, find the broken colour and use this in large proportions, especially where the dyed colours are particularly strident. When two contrasting colours which are not complementaries are used, neutral grey, buff, brown and green should be introduced and also, wherever possible, more hues which are near to the contrasting colours on the spectrum.

For your guidance I list below the natural complementaries. I have split the spectrum colours a little differently from the way they are usually shown so that all the dyed colours are included: red and blue-green; yellow-red (orange) and blue; yellow and purple-blue (violet); green-yellow (lime) and purple; green and red-purple (magenta).

Arrangements made entirely from dyed flowers and other perpetuelles are lifeless! This is perhaps surprising in view of the terrific amount of colour employed, but there is no doubt in my mind that the dyeing drowns some essential quality. I am convinced that this ghost quality is the absence of colour gradation from the materials. There is a monotonous sameness about the whole stem. Therefore, the arranger should aim to introduce other materials to bring back that quality into the finished arrangement. The more variety there is in a mixed arrangement the more surely is success guaranteed. One tone should lead to the next, up or down the colour scale.

Another important thing is to learn to appreciate the colour in the naturally coloured materials themselves, a point too often overlooked. For example, all yellow helichrysums are far from having the same colour value.

I find that it helps me considerably to divide the materials into colour groups before I begin to assemble them. I suggested earlier that this should begin as far back as the harvesting. But for the arranger who intends to market the finished product on a fairly large scale, my advice is to begin with the great quantities of helichrysum that are sure to be needed. Make these the pivot round which the rest will revolve. Divide the reds into rosy-reds, orange-reds, bronze-reds; the yellows into cream and primrose, gold and orange-gold; and back to the rosy-reds to divide them into palest pinks and the deepest carmines.

In the home we can go about things a little more quietly. You may perhaps like to have a large mass arrangement of soft broken colours in the drawing room and a gay 'won't you please come in' piece in the hall. It is all a matter of colour. I think that with dried arrangements it is colour, or lack of colour, first and design second, for it is impossible to plan the nature of the arrangement until the colours have been decided upon.

First select the container and take a colour guide from that. By so doing, unexpected colour harmonies often reward the arranger. For instance, in a copper vessel there are often many colours to be seen, purple, green as well as the basic near-orange of the metal.

Incidentally, metal containers are good for dried materials. For example, if in a copper jug we arrange orange physalis, helichrysum, apricot tinted limonium, beech leaves and the bare but lovely orange stems of willow and dogwood, we shall find that the copper will absorb much of the orange from the materials yet will, at the same time, impart some of its own gleam to them, giving them warmth.

A monochromatic harmony, where we strive to use all materials of one hue; or an analogous harmony in which we use colours that are near each other in the spectrum, often results in greater colour value than if the container is of a different hue. For example if, instead of the near-copper hues of the materials mentioned above, we decided to use the near-complementary blue (I say near-complementary because orange is the natural complement of blue and I have substituted copper for orange), we should find that the colour harmony had a different value. The first, of the greater impact, might look better in the hall, while the arrangement with the complementary blues, still in copper, might be more suitable for the living room where a more restful harmony strikes the correct note. Of course, the colours that you use should always harmonise with the furnishings.

I once wanted something in blue-grey that would make a pleasant 'permanent' table decoration and 'tie-in' with the pewter about the room and on the table. Blue-grey perpetuelles can look dull, especially in winter, so—as I have discovered that one can sometimes take chances with patterned containers when using these more than when arranging fresh flowers—I selected a Japanese rice bowl. The white was not pure and had just a wash-day hint of blue. The overlying pattern, blue and terra-cotta, matched the carpet and gave me a near-complementary theme to play

113

with. Frankly, I was quite unprepared for the full depth of blue colour ultimately to be seen. This certainly was not dull! The perpetuelles were echinops, lavender and limonium of which only the first was really blue, the others inclined to the violet and were, as you can tell, analogous. With them I arranged a contrast, white limonium which I knew would make the blue seem even bluer.

The amount of dyed materials I use personally is minimal. I draw on them in quantity only if I have to arrange perpetuelles for some special occasion outside my home. At home I use only natural plant material but when I make arrangements as gifts I do sometimes add a little artificial colour, usually because I know that it will be appreciated by the person to whom I am going to give the flowers.

Examples of dyed perpetuelles I use are as follows. Dyed grevillea keeps its olive-grey leaf surface colour but takes on the dye underneath and in its stems. I find this orange dyed foliage useful. It is dull enough to look natural, many undyed leaves—some rhododendron for instance—have similar hues underneath, and it matches and harmonises with a colour present in so many perpetuelles, helichrysum, gomphrena, physalis, celosia and some gourds for example.

Very occasionally I use dyed grasses but again, only those that conceivably might be natural, greens, orange or yellow. Dyed shadow leaves, browns in particular, are useful for filling in the back and base of some arrangements without making them dense or heavy. I use these in vivid colours for party and Christmas decorations.

Fortunately for those who abhor dyed plant materials of any kind there are many which retain much of their natural hue. One point to bear in mind is that because of their dry texture they tend to absorb light rather than to reflect it, hence the wisdom of using plenty of white and light yellow, and the reason for using white or light-coloured containers for pastel tinted arrangements. Browns can go with browns but the light summer hues look best with a companion colour.

Over the years I have been enchanted with the blue of delphiniums and hydrangeas, so specially welcome because none of the cheerful, colourful true everlastings contribute this colour.

The great thing for the home decorator of course, is to find colours which will suit the furnishings. I think that there are sufficient hues among the many perpetuelles to make this possible. However, even if the idea of drying a lot of non-everlastings in a dessicant does not appeal, it might prove worth while to use this method just to dry sufficient flowers of a certain colour to match the decor. These could be arranged among neutral and broken colours.

## Home Dyeing

Many readers write to ask me for methods of dyeing dried materials—in particular grasses—in small quantities, and I have to admit that I cannot help them as much as I would like. For while this can be done economically and practically on a large scale, dyeing presents problems when it has to be done in the home and it is never really absolutely successful.

In the first place, it is often difficult to buy small quantities of commercial plant dyes and when these are used it is necessary not only to steep but sometimes to heat the materials, often for lengthy periods in extremely large vessels. In this case, a separate building is almost essential.

However, like myself, some of my readers have experimented with domestic dyes and although the results are often unpredictable they are not offensive and the dyed perpetuelles can be used.

Once when I had quickly to produce gnaphaliums of a certain colour for a special purpose, in desperation I tried the only dye in the house, Easter egg colourant. I followed the directions for mixing and dipped the flower heads in the hot dye instead of boiling them and this proved quite satisfactory.

In the case of these flowers and other white or light hued blooms it is sometimes possible to give them the dye in their drinking water, made warm not hot, while the flowers are still in a fresh state. When the petals show the dye colour the flowers can then be taken out and dried in the usual way. But I fear that this is very much a case for personal experimentation.

Skeletonised leaves will take ink as well as egg colourant as a dye.

# CHAPTER 10

# Assembly

In the arrangement of both dried and preserved materials one has to take a step away from the actual craft of flower arrangement as it is usually understood or interpreted by the amateur, towards floristry as practised by the professional. For this reason I feel it is important to discuss the subject of assembly before that of arrangement. Obviously the two will overlap.

It is possible to concentrate on flower arrangement alone and to decline the use of any artifice either in colour or assembly, but this really is going the hard way about it! Those arrangers who hope to make some financial gain from the cultivation and subsequent arrangement of dried materials need some elementary knowledge of floristry, for assembly of parts into an artificial whole is a necessity.

The greatest difference between arrangement and floristry lies in the use of wire, either as a false stem or support. Wire is usually sold by weight. It varies from $3\frac{1}{2}$ to 18in in length and is done up in bundles, or on reels for uncut wire. The thickness of the individual wires is known by the 'gauge' number, the smaller the number the thicker the wire. The gauges range from 16 to 30 in the cut wires.

There are many kinds of reel wire. 'Silver', used mainly for wiring very delicate stems or for binding fine stems together is obtainable in 28, 30, 32, 34 and 36 gauges. Blue reel wire, slightly tougher, comes in 24, 26, 28, 30 and 32 gauges. Green or white plastic covered wire is usually obtainable in 28 gauge.

A golden rule should always be: use as few wires as possible. When they are used they should never be visible. The size of wire to be used depends on what kind of flower it is and how it is to be used. Much depends also on the weight or density of the flower. A large helichrysum would need a stronger wire than a dainty acroclinium. For a guide, 18 gauge wire should be used for only the thickest flower stems and where some even thicker materials have to be wired it is possible to use two or three 18g wires together. For medium stems use 20-22g; 22-28g for thin stems. If the wire is right it will be possible to use it without undue pressure.

## Wiring

Wires are used chiefly as a support to prevent the bloom being broken from its stem. For dried flowers a wire can take the place of a stem.

When a flower is to retain its stem, one end of the support wire is inserted into the stem just below the bloom head and pushed into it until it meets the hard seed box within the petals. The wire is then twisted a few times round the stem until it reached the base. The flower stem should never be twisted round the wire. Except on close inspection the wire should not show. It should lie quite flat to the stem. When it is taken down the stem it should not go round and round it in a tight spiral. Instead the spirals should be very long drawn out.

This is one method, but wherever possible the wire

118

should be inserted up through the centre of the stem until it reaches the seed box, thus making it invisible. This is a simple operation when hollow-stemmed flowers are to be wired.

When a wire is used as a substitute for a stem there are two methods which can be used according to the type of flower. For heads of helichrysums which have no stem portion at all, make a small crook at one end of the wire. Pass the other end through the very centre of the flower, pointing downwards, and pull gently until the loop of the crook is embedded in the flower's centre and partly concealed by it. All daisy-like and open flowers can be wired this way.

For other flowers, large delphinium florets, for example, take a wire, thin for small flowers, thicker for large blooms, but remember that no dried bloom is as heavy as a fresh one, pass it through the base of the bloom, through its seed box or thickest part until there are equal lengths on each side. Bend these down and twist them once round each other to form a 'double-leg'.

If the petals are likely to drop or if there is no seed box below the petals, pass the wire through the flower just above the junction of the stem and bloom.

Not only must the stem, leaves or blooms sometimes be given support, but wires are often needed either to add length to a stem or, and especially if it is not a rigid or tough stem, to enable one to insert it into the container. This method of applying wires is known as 'mounting' and it is an important operation for the arranger of dried materials since so many things have either to be lengthened or given false stems, or 'helped'.

In many cases this is really simple. For instance, if you want to make a piece of limonium longer than it is, often all that is necessary is to insert an 18g wire (or two or three together if the piece is very long and heavy) as far up the stem as it will go. But more often the mount has to be applied outside the stem.

The leg made by the mounting wire may be single or double. A double-leg forms a firm anchorage but it is sometimes a nuisance to arrange unless these are taped or bound as one.

## Single-legged mount

Mounting is done this way. Take the material to be treated in one hand. Hold the wire in the other. Bend one end of it over the index finger to form a loop about an inch in length. Lay the loop against the wired stem (alternatively, against any tough stem which may not need wiring, only mounting), leaving the short end of the loop protruding beyond the base of the stem for a little way. Firmly hold the loop in position against the stem as you take the long end of wire and pass it twice round the stem, taking in the short leg of wire as it goes. This tiny short end gives you something other than the stem alone to put pressure on. Bring the long end down so that it forms a continuation of the stem.

## Double-legged mount

Place a wire at the back of a wired stem so that there are equal portions on each side of the stem. Or, alternatively, first bend the wire hair-pin fashion and place the loop of the 'hair-pin' behind the stem. In either case, bring the right-hand length of wire over the left and pass it round the stem two or three times.

Having explained the fundamentals of wiring and mounting flowers, I suggest that I go back to the second chapter and take the various items as they occur so that there shall be no likelihood of any important point overlooked.

AMMOBIUM improves by being broken down into short stemmed flowers. To give these height they should be mounted on single-legs. If you divide the tall branching stems very carefully you can usually take away side stems and leave one tall central stem. I find that I can often bunch five or seven or so flowers together and mount these as one unit. To do this, arrange the flowers in your hand first in such a way that the blooms are 'stepped', each having its own space with one bloom at the top of the group. Hold the stems together firmly and mount them all with the same wire. An alternative to mounting is to wire the stems internally when they are fresh, but even so you may have to shorten or lengthen when you come actually to arrange them.

ANAPHALIS and GNAPHALIUM. The garden anaphalis and the commercial gnaphalium look well when set in little round trusses of bloom, polyanthus-like. The tiny flower stems, petioles, are sometimes extremely brittle. It is best to pull the flower clusters from the main head so that three or more tiny blooms share one little stalk. Many of these clusters can then be placed, heads level, round a centre core consisting of an inch or more of tougher but not much thicker stalk. These stems should then be bound togehter with fine reel wire.

Alternatively, the little clusters can be grouped round a true centre point, for example a small cone, ready mounted. These then would form a posy round which small leaves, each individually mounted, can be arranged like a collar. Such posies can be used in the same way as a large individual bloom.

121

It is quite easy, though time-consuming, to make small bunches of either of these flowers into spikes of bloom, resembling mullein more than anything else. Sometimes a contrasting colour helps to create a more natural effect or, failing this, helps with the planned colour harmony. For example a spire of blue-dyed gnaphalium can have each 'flower' made with a white centre, delphinium-like. Garden anaphalis can be dyed black and used as a centre, bee-like as in delphiniums, in a ring of white naturally coloured blooms.

## Making spikes

The following method is a basic one and can be employed not only for bunch anaphalis and gnaphalium, as I have suggested, but also for other blooms, fruits and leaves.

Every individual bloom, every little bunch of materials, every leaf, whatever you use, should first be mounted on a fine, short, wire, double-legged method. Some materials you may want to use, poppies for example, often can be adequately wired by insertion instead of leg-mounting.

Prepare the main stem by covering a slender cane or willow, privet or lilac wand, or bind several long heavy wires together. Cover the stem by taping it either with proper florist's tape or with 'stem green' crepe paper made into binding tape by cutting it into $\frac{1}{2}$in strips, right through several thicknesses of the folded paper.

## Taping a cane

Begin at the top of the cane, first binding a piece over the end in the same way as one places a bandage over the end of a thumb. Then, taking the tape round and round the cane in tight spirals, one edge of the tape carefully covering the edge of the piece above it, work to the base. Fasten off securely by using a little adhesive tape. The finished 'stem' should look as smooth as possible. The tape will help the mounted materials stay in place.

## Assembling the spike

Grade the materials so that you can put the smallest at the tip and work down the spike towards the largest. Put the smallest in position. Twist the thin wire with which it is mounted twice or thrice round the foundation so that it is well secured and will stay firmly in place. Cut away any surplus wire or, if it is only a short length, smooth it down against the foundation but do not go on twisting it round and round or a heavy, ugly spike will be the result. I prefer to trim the wires away.

As the first piece is mounted to the foundation, attach also the end of the tape. If you leave this rolled up it will be easier to work with. Take the tape round the foundation so that it hides the wiring and the stem end or ends of the piece just applied. Do not make this taping bulky, it is for neatening purpose only and twice round the foundation should be enough; once round might be all that is needed in some cases.

Next, place the other piece, a little to the right or left of the first piece and, of course, a little below. Cover the wired stem of each piece with tape as work proceeds. Go on adding the pieces but increase their numbers as you reach the lower portions of the spike to give it a heavier or thicker base. It may be necessary to arrange the lower pieces so that they stand away from the foundation a little.

If you want to make very fine spikes of little flowers it may not be necessary to use tape. Instead, use the flowers themselves to cover the mounting wires of any placed above them.

It is possible to make some spikes of certain materials without using any wires at all. It all depends upon the materials used, which should be tough but not brittle. They need to be things which have an inch or more of stem; some leaves can be done this way. If the stems are too short they cannot be bound in firmly and so will not stay in place. Just lay the stem on the foundation and tape in place.

If you wish, a few leaves of some kind can be mounted at the base of a flower spike. Be sure always to leave enough bare portion for arrangement. The spike can always be mounted on a false stem if it appears to be not quite tall enough.

Bare branches can be used to display individual blooms of both anaphalis and gnaphalium, which can be fixed on the branches as though they were its blossom. Single flowers can be set at or near the branch tips with clusters of three or more in the axils of branches and lower down the stems. Any colourless fixative will do to secure them but make sure that all the stem is out from the flower so that it sits well on its new branch. Garden anaphalis can be dyed with household dyes. Pink blooms make good 'blossom'.

GOMPHRENA. You can treat gomphrena in any of the ways described above. It makes an interesting spike but I find it is not an easy stem to wire. One likes to retain its own stems where possible and I find that it is best to reinforce the natural stem. To do this, take a fine wire up to just below the bloom and push the end in it. This never penetrates far but try to make it hold, no matter how slightly. Then, holding this wire (a rose wire is good for this because it is dark in colour) close to the stem, take another wire and apply this, single-legged method, about half-way up the stem. Twist its long end slowly down to the base of the stem, taking in the first wire to be applied as it encircles

*Page 125* Mounted on a gilt card, helipterums, fragments of
lonas, limonium, thuja and grasses. The stem ends, saved from
the grasses, are mounted separately (p149)

*Page 126* Made in the lid of a powder box, which also protects them from dust, helipterum with pressed fern and geranium leaves, violas and individual florets of limonium (p152)

the flower stem. Alternatively, wire the stems as described in the first chapter.

HELICHRYSUMS and other daisy-like flowers. As I explained at the beginning of this book, it is sometimes best to wire flowers while they are still fresh and in the case of the strawflowers this is best done by taking the bloom with only an inch or two of stem. While this is still moist and soft, insert a wire and dry the flowers ready wired.

When these flowers are bought they are usually already beheaded and dried, in which state they are not very easy to wire because their tissues have become so tough and resistant. They can be wired and mounted in the same operation, as described earlier, by inserting a crooked wire down through the flowers' centres. But there is one difficulty here. Because the flowers are so hard to penetrate, one tends to take a thick 18g wire for this purpose. But this particular gauge is too rigid as a flower stem for these daisies, which are themselves a little too stiff in appearance. A lighter wire 20 or 22g gives a 'stem' a little more suppleness.

To aid wiring it is worth spending a little more time over the operation and first to pierce the centre with a long, strong pin, following through at once with the wire end.

Because these flowers are wired and mounted on false stems at one and the same time, when they are to be arranged it will be sufficient merely to insert their 'stems' in the usual way. However, the arranger must take care or the uncovered wires will give a thin, harsh look to the finished arrangement. And anyway, it is a pity to use a good wire for one purpose only when it could serve two.

To fill in the lower parts of an arrangement at the same time as you place flowers in the higher levels, screen and camouflage the stem wire by placing some other material against it and mount this to it. For instance, it is a simple

127

matter to lay two or three bracken fronds, single fronds not whole ferns, a spray of *Limonium latifolium*, a group of shorter grasses, on the wire as arrangement progresses. You will soon learn where many or where few of these applied fillers are needed. I find that this saves me much time both in arrangement and wiring.

## Making stems from straws

There is no doubt that wires are convenient and quick to use but they are not the loveliest things for flower stems. Where it is possible to substitute a wire stem by a false stem of some kinder or more appropriate material, it is advisable to do so for then the flowers will take on a softer and more natural appearance. Furthermore such stems will not need to be hidden. (See plate p89.)

This is where the saved grasses and the straws come in useful! These will make clean, bright, easily arranged stems for helichrysums and all other strawdaisies. Stems or straws cut from dyed grasses will also add a little extra colour especially if you match them to the flowers, rosy helipterums with carmine stems of rye grass are examples.

Once again, the hole must be pre-pierced. If a whole grass is to be used, insert its stem end in first and then gently pull it through towards its flower head. Cut this so that the merest portion is left, enough for a 'stopper' and then pull it down into the centre of the flower.

One way of inserting a straw through a tough flower is to use a small piece of wire inserted in the end of the straw. After pre-piercing, push the wire through the flower and it will draw the straw after it.

These straw-stemmed flowers often hang much more gracefully than any others, especially if the straw tapers. You can save these for the edges and extremities of an arrangement and use stiff-stemmed flowers, including wire-stemmed, in the centre where their rigidity is not such a disadvantage.

If you have neither wires nor straws you can use pipe-cleaners in the same way. These make excellent stems although they are more expensive than the other kinds. If they are to act as stems for downy materials they will need no camouflaging but they do look a little odd supporting crisp orange or red helichrysums yet they suit the white and cream kinds. Pipe cleaners have the advantage of being malleable so that attractive curving stems can be made.

HELIPTERUMS, acroclinium. These little strawdaisies will retain their stems better than the helichrysums and they can be wired by pushing and then spiralling it down the stem. Take care when you do this that you do not twist the stem, an easy thing to do with this particular flower. If it is necessary to wire helipterums follow the directions for helichrysums.

HELIPTERUM, rhodanthe. These do need slightly different treatment. I find that the stem remains tough and the blooms are seldom severed from it. However, the stems are also brittle and are sometimes a little difficult to mount with either single or double legs unless the stem base, against which the wires will be pressed, is first reinforced. Usually all that is necessary is to insert one of the finest wires up inside the stem as far as it will go. This method can also be used to lengthen the stems.

*LIMONIUM SINUATUM.* Fortunately this is a long-stemmed stout flower and when used perfectly naturally is seldom in need of support. However, the stems left just as they are gathered are often far too branching to arrange

129

effectively and, in any case, to use them exactly as they grow would be uneconomic because not all of the flower could be seen properly.

Side stems should be removed and used separately. These often have a curved, spicate shape which I find very useful for placing at the extremities of an arrangement to give it some shape and movement.

On most stems also there are little clusters which, as they are small and not distinctively shaped, are relatively unimportant to the stem as a whole. These can be grouped together to make a more important colour mass or, they can be posied in any of the ways discussed earlier. For tiny arrangements, they can be divided into their sections and each of these can then be wired and mounted separately.

The stems can be lengthened by inserting a wire and this is easier, as you would expect, when the flower is freshly gathered. If you intend making some tall arrangements I would recommend that you wire some stems ready while this is easy to do. Later, if they are too dry and too tough to allow for insertion, mount the stems by the single-legged method.

In very tall arrangements it will be necessary to use the double-legged method and with strong wires, possibly with two or more kept together. Really tall, heavy stems can also be mounted by splicing them to a thin cane or twig.

For such arrangements also, it saves much time and trouble, if a few limonium are placed in a dainty bunch, roughly triangular in outline, their tips at various levels. Their stem ends should then be trimmed roughly level and mounted. Two or more wires may have to be used together.

LIMONIUMS. Most of the foregoing remarks apply to any other limonium which may be used, the only differences being that some, such as *L. latifolium*, are differently shaped and so serve a slightly different decorative purpose. I use these daintier kinds for masking the stem wires of other flowers in the manner described in the section on helichrysum.

LONAS. These have really tough little stems which offer no problem for mounting.

XERANTHEMUM. The same applies to these straw-daisies as to lonas, above.

ACHILLEA. Large heads of *A. filipendulina* can be divided into smaller sections and the new-sized flowers mounted on long single-legged mounts if they are to be used in arrangements. I find this a useful thing to do, especially when I am short of dense yellow flowers as opposed to daisy-eyed kinds. This achillea looks well in swags.

*ACHILLEA PTARMICA.* As well as being arranged as a flower in its own right, the sneezewort can also be used in the same way as described for anaphalis.

*CYNARA CARDUNCULUS* and others. These flowers may need really strong false stems. Attach them as follows.

## Splicing stems

To heighten a large and heavy stem, splicing should be employed. This consists merely in fastening a cane or thin stick to the end of the stem. Bear in mind that this lower false stem must always be stronger than the upright portion attached to it.

Sometimes it is possible to insert the stronger portion, which may be thinner, inside the upper stem but even so, I have always found that where the base is thinner some problems do occur. Usually what happens is that it becomes difficult to get the whole piece to stay in place just as it should. The thin base tends to make the flower swing round.

It is best to lay 1-2in of the top of the lower portion, to the bottom 1-2in of the base of the stem and bind them firmly together with adhesive tape.

Heavy stems such as amaranthus and others which are to be pendulous in arrangement, are more easily placed if they are spliced to thicker stems or mounted on strong wires. They can then first be set at the correct angle and arranged accordingly.

## Mounting and wiring leaves

Individual leaves can be mounted on wires or canes or other false stems according to their size and the way they are to be used.

When they are mounted on wires this can be done by using the single-legged mount and placing the loop behind the leaf, just above the junction of stem and leaf. The top of the loop should rest on the base of the leaf and the wire should run each side of the short stem. To mount the leaf, take the long wire round the stem as near to its top as possible without damaging the leaf itself and also round the short stem.

Naturally, the larger the leaf the heavier the wire needed to support it but try to keep the wire as inconspicuous as possible. Small leaves such as shrubby senecio, ivy or perhaps shadow leaves of holly will need only very light and fine wires.

Some leaves look well and are often more useful if they are mounted in threes, clover leaf fashion. Not all leaves will need to be attached to some other mount but can be arranged with their wire forming the stem, just like the flowers, but where two or more are joined together their wires are combined to make the main stem. This is done quite simply. Always grade them, first so that small and tapering specimens may be set at the tips.

Lay the first leaf in position on the table. Place another to the left of it and a little lower. Keep the wire mounts or false stems parallel to each other. Never twist them round each other or the result will be most cumbersome. Instead bind them together with very fine reel wire or you can tape them. Next, place a leaf to the right of the second leaf and slightly lower. Bind the stems. As more leaves are added alternately, the main stem becomes firm. When sufficient leaves have been mounted the spray itself can be given a false stem should this be necessary.

You can mount leaves on a long stem in the same manner as is used for making a spike of flowers. In this case though, the leaves will not need to be arranged all round the main stem, unless of course this is the purpose of the operation.

It is often desirable to arrange wide-spreading graceful sprays of leaves in an outsize decoration, to soften the outline or perhaps to provide a silhouette. If this is done skillfully and with imagination, and by studying natural growth, the result can be quite charming.

Use a ready made natural foundation. Leafless beech twigs are excellent because they grow flat and yet are graceful. They also have clean brown dainty stems. Pointed buds are an asset too, for if these are laid over the mounted leaf they not only help to hide the joint but they also act as a leaf stem.

Always grade the leaves for size. Lay a leaf flat against the twig, cut the base of the leaf stem butts on the slant should they be rounded or not likely to lie flat. Begin

133

mounting the leaves always at the tip of a branch or side-branch and place it behind a bud so that the stem itself is just below the bud.

The quickest and most effective way to fix the leaves is with a colourless adhesive. Lay the branch flat on a table and weight the leaves down as they are arranged.

Sometimes one finds good leaves which do not have useful stems by which they can be easily mounted. Depending upon their texture it might be possible either to pierce them or to stitch them. I use the first method for mounting round leaves such as can be stripped from some types of eucalyptus whose foliage grows in whorls round the stem.

To do this, first I push a thin wire through the leaf from front to back at a point near its base and where I think that the tissues are strong. I then bring these two legs together each flat against its side of the leaf. It is now possible to mount the leaf, using either the single- or double-legged method and treating the first wire as though it were the true stem. Usually, leaves treated this way look better if the wires are taped.

To stitch the leaf, turn it so that its underside is uppermost and note its midrib or centre vein. Pass a wire through the leaf on each side of this, bring the ends down and out to the upper surface just above the base of the leaf. Bend these back to form the stem. Carefully twist one round the other.

## Wiring ferns

Often it is possible to buy large fronds of preserved, dyed or bleached adiantum fern. This quite beautiful plant, native to New Zealand and other countries can be used without any special attention except for one thing. The stems are inclined to snap when pressure is exerted on them and as you often want these fronds to curve this can be annoying.

As the natural stem of this and other adiantums is black and very wiry in appearance, one can take advantage of this fact and wire the fronds with a dark wire all along this stem, winding it between the junction of laterals and main stem. Begin at the stem end and work towards the tip. Later lengthen and mount by applying a wire to the portion of stem end already reinforced.

Another way the fern can be mounted without danger of its stem snapping is to lay a strong wire along its stem on the underside of the frond and to cover this with a clear adhesive tape from one end to the other. This method can also be used with any frail leaves. As with all other ferns, laterals and sections of fronds can be used. Mount these with single-leg fine wires.

Unless they are to be used in an outsize arrangement and have been pressed or otherwise preserved with this end in view, bracken fronds are best removed from the main stem. Each of these side shoots is a perfect fern frond in itself and is quite large enough for most requirements. In any case, the fronds on one stem vary in size. They are easily lengthened by either splicing or wire-mounting.

Side fronds do not have much stem which means that the lowest of the even smaller fronds will have to be stripped off the stem for an inch or so in order that it can be properly mounted. To mount, it is usually best to take a long wire and make a double-legged mount, placing the loop at the top of the stripped portion of the stem so that it just rests against the fern itself.

The tiny sub-ferns stripped from bracken and all other kinds of ferns are well worth saving. I like to press them for use in flower pictures. They can also be grouped together in a variety of ways, as a fan, a star and mounted at the lower part of some mount wire holding a flower.

Many of these tiniest of all fronds are still large enough to be used in small arrangements. Whenever you are mounting two or more together, overlap their bases, don't bother to strip these tiny 'ferns', and hold them all together firmly between finger and thumb while the loop of a double-legged mount is placed behind them. When one leg is passed round, as the ferns are being mounted, make sure that these bases are being embraced and held quite firm by the mount wire.

## Wiring and mounting cones

Once again, the weight of the wire will depend upon the size of the cone to be treated. Very large specimens will need not only wiring by an 18g wire but also another one, double-leg, for mounting. Tiny cones, including larch, can often be mounted on rose wires but this really depends on how they are to be used.

The real problem with most cones is that they have no stem portion and yet, when this does exist we find it best to wire them and mount them at the same time by easing the wire in between the scales on the lower portion of the cone. You often have to do this quite roughly to get the wire right down inside the scales near the centre. The nearer to the base you do this the better poised the cone will be. Leave roughly equal portions of wire on each side as the wire is taken round inside the cone. You can then bring these down under the cone where they can be twisted once round each other to form a 'stem'.

## Making garlands and ropes or swags of cones

I always like to grade all the cones if I am using a mix-

ture, so that the very smallest ones can be used at the extremes. Even so, small cones are also bunched together and
used among the large ones. This prevents them from looking too 'zoned'. (See plate p107.)

It is necessary also to 'face' cones, that is, to bend their
wires so that they will stand up from the design which has
to be flat if it is to lie or hang well. This is quite simple
and you can do it as assembly progresses.

First have everything wired, including a great number
of leaves for the backing. These also should be mounted.
Lay the smallest leaf on the table. Arrange first the smallest
cone and then one or two more until the centre of the leaf
is covered and just the tip shows beyond the first cone.
Keep all mount wires straight at first. Take the mount wire
of the leaf and bring this round across the other wires and
back round again, thus pinning them or binding them together. Take this wire round twice and then straighten it
out alongside the others.

Next, slip another leaf at the back, its tip reaching about
halfway up the other leaf. Do not lift the 'rope' up to see to
this, it should be possible to do all of this work with the
'rope' lying on the table. Hold the leaf-mount wire against
the back of the others while you arrange the other cones
and repeat the process as soon as you see that you have covered the leaf area. Continue, gradually adding large leaves
and cones if you are making a tapered rope, keeping them
even if the rope is to be the same thickness throughout.
When it is long enough, neaten the wires and tape them.

To make a garland, repeat this process using a ring of
strong wire to lie between the leaves and the cones. (See
plate p107.)

You can mix the ingredients for this type of design as
much as you wish. It is not essential to use only cones. I use,
nuts of all kinds, teasels, thistles, berry-like seed heads of

**137**

tutsan or hypericum, small lotus and other seed heads, poppies of all sizes, conkers and sweet chestnut burrs, brown achillea and sedum heads to mention only a few.

If you want to make a 'drape' over a mirror, a mantelpiece, a door, or something of that nature, make the swag in three sections, one for each side and one, or two halves with a centre knot, to join them.

If you leave the ends long, tape them and then curve them, you can make a good strong ring from which to suspend the rope.

*MAKING CONE ROSES*. Some of the large cones of cedars when really mature (they take two years to reach this state) will when placed in a warm room break up so that their scales can be handled individually. From these, cone 'roses' can be made.

For small and somewhat compact roses one can use the method described for honesty but for wider, flatter 'Carmen' roses (p142) one must use a circle of stiff fabric as a backing. Cut the circle a little smaller than the ultimate diameter of the rose. Mount it by doubling a wire hairpin-fashion and threading it through the centre of the material. Twist the two equal legs of wire one round the other directly below the material, but keep this flat, and cover them with stem tape. Stand this stem in a container deep enough for the fabric to rest on its rim and lie flat.

Beginning at the outer edge, lay the first ring of scales in place using a little adhesive on the base of each Experiment a little before using the adhesive to ensure that the scales are curving the correct way and that they lie in such a way that the adhesive will make contact with the fabric without being pressed. Work towards the centre, laying concentric circles until the heart of the rose is reached. At this point fix a smaller cone.

It is possible to make similar roses by using all kinds of other materials, small preserved or pressed leaves for instance, or even the fallen seed scales of elm. This is a field in which experiment is both rewarding and entertaining.

Where there exists a thick stem or base cut this away. Alternatively, use the stem end or the base as the 'petal' tip.

CYCAS LEAVES. Three or five leaves can be arranged in a fan, fastened to one common stem and used as a background to other materials. This is a good way of using a narrow necked container. The one stem will take so much less room than five. First mount the leaves on 18g wires and then either bind the mounts together with reel wire or, if they are to be arranged high, mount them on a false stem.

If you want to curve the whole leaf, take a long wire, 22g will probably be best, twist one end round the short cycas stem, then wind it right down to the tip of the leaf—I say down because you will find it easiest to hold the leaf upside down for this treatment. As you spiral the wire round the stem, take it between each leaflet or every other leaflet. Make sure that you clear them and do not hold them down with the wire. Cut away the surplus wire at the leaf tip. If you wire very long leaves, it may be necessary to join the wires mid-leaf. Once it is wired like this, you can curve the leaf quite considerably.

Leaves can be divided down the midrib and made into two 'ostrich feathers'. These then form attractive ends for garlands and swags. The smaller leaves are easier to slice through than the large. Start from the base of the stem and with a sharp knife, split the midrib down the centre. If when the 'feathers' are arranged you see that the split midrib is on the under edge of the leaf, it will fall more gracefully.

## Mounting gourds

If there is no stem on the gourd it will have to be mounted on an 18g wire. If the top of the gourd is to be the part which is 'faced', the wire should be passed through the gourd near its base. Push it through until there are roughly equal lengths of wire on each side, bring these down to below the gourd and twist them round each other to make the stem.

If the gourd is to be displayed in 'profile', some of the pear-shaped and bottle kinds look good this way, simply pierce the wire into the gourd on the other, hidden, side.

This sounds quite easy, but, unfortunately, the skin of a ripe gourd is so hard that it is difficult to penetrate, and really the best way of making a hole so that the wire can be pushed through it to use a red hot awl or steel knitting needle. Never pierce more fruits than are needed at the moment, because those that are injured do not last so long as those which are intact.

Gourds may be used in swags as well as in arrangements. One simple way of mounting a large gourd is to use a golf tee. Arrange the gourd as you want it and fix it to the tee with an adhesive. Later, when it has dried, mount the tee.

## Grasses

When arranging an outsize decoration, it is often better to bunch the grasses rather than to try to arrange them individually. Take care that you vary the stem lengths so that all the heads are not at one level. Tie them and either mount them on a strong wire or to a long false stem, depending on their place in the arrangement.

# Wiring and mounting hydrangeas

If you intend to keep the heads intact try to wire their stems before drying. Heads may be divided into sections and even into individuals. If the latter are not to be pressed for pictures, wire these by inserting a fine wire inside the stem as far as it will go.

Sometimes hydrangeas tend to become brittle after drying and then portions separated from the main cluster are difficult to mount without shattering the flowers. Mount them as follows.

Lay a fine wire parallel to the short stem. Push its tip up into the flower cluster, or if a single flower is being mounted, as far as the top of the stem but not into the flower. Hold the wire in place with the finger and thumb of one hand, close to the top of the stem. Gently take the lower portion round the short stem spiralling it to its base. Straighten the remaining wire. If necessary the wired stem can be taped with narrowed (halved) tape.

If you wish to use individual florets, and some of the large blue ones can be both useful and attractive in mixed arrangements, use a fine straw as a false stem. Dip the top inch or so in colourless adhesive and simply place it against the fine, short hydrangea stem. Allow to dry before arrangement. Use this method for mounting other fragile flowers, particularly those which have been dried in a dessicant, because this way handling is at a minimum.

A way to wire full heads with short stems is as follows. Pass a suitable wire, possibly 22g, up through the centre of the flower cluster, between and among the stems, but without piercing either them or the flowers. Bring the wire up beyond the cluster for about an inch or so and then turn the tip back to make a loop of about a half inch. Gently pull the wire back down again until you can feel that the

141

loop is straddling the tiny stems hidden inside the flower cluster. It should hook over them. Lay the visible portion of wire flush against the stem below the flowers and cover the two with tape, binding them closely together. Take the tape to the base of the wire if this is likely to be seen in arrangement.

## *Lunaria or honesty*

Individual 'moons' can be mounted on fine wires and made into 'flowers'. Group them round a suitable centre-piece, a tiny cone, a yellow helichrysum bud or a nigella seed head, also mounted. Bind all the mount 'stems' neatly together. Do not twist them one round the other or they will be bulky and ugly. Place a wire alongside these mount wires and tape all together to make a neat stem. (See plate p35.)

'Roses' can be made by using a small mounted cone as the 'core'. Remove the tiny stem from the base of the honesty moons and push each moon down in the spaces between the scales. These should hold quite firm but if you are doubt-ful, put the slightest touch of adhesive on the honesty first.

For arrangements on a small scale, honesty stems should be divided and the small laterals used after they have been mounted on false stems or wire mounts.

I find small bunches, made by grouping detached moons together, useful in some swags and ropes, especially when I make these of grey, silver and other light-toned materials. These can also be wired and grouped three together, clover-leaf fashion, to place behind some other perpetuelle such as a phlomis seed head.

It is also possible to make quite large 'double' blooms by using a circular piece of paper or strong gauze as a founda-tion and fixing the moons to this with a clear adhesive. Be-

*Page 143* A Byzantine cone
is made on a base of dry
Oasis shaped to fit the
goblet. First a curving
line of beech mast is in-
serted, small stems hold
quite firm; larch cones,
wire mounted, are ar-
ranged on one side, wider
sedum heads flanked by
grey lupin pods on the
other. The cones continue
down and around the rim.
A yucca seed pod forms
the apex. Camphor buds
are flanked by phlomis
seed heads, fragments of
rush and clusters of
*Hypericum androsaemum*
berries fill the space
between (pp154-7)

*Page 144* The block of dry Oasis used as stem holder has been placed on the container so that it projects over the rim as well as above it. Low lying flowers are arranged upside down in the projecting portion (p159)

gin making the outer circle of petals first. These should overlap the foundation by about half their petal length. Work, placing the honesty in concentric circles, until the centre is reached and finish this off with a suitable item. A soft cone, a nigella seed head, a tiny head of lonas or achillea—both yellow—are examples. Mount the foundation before beginning to fix the honesty.

## Poppy seed heads

While the large poppy heads are usually considered to be the most decorative, the dried-flower arranger will find that all sizes from all species and varieties can be used in many ways.

The large ones are usually imported and have been used at some time for obtaining opium! You can see the cut across the side of the capsule. When you arrange or mount these heads, bear this cut in mind and arrange the poppy accordingly.

I grow great quantities of the so-called opium poppy, *Papaver somniferum*, which is listed by most seedsmen and which contains some lovely varieties of great blowzy flowers, paeony and carnation-shaped as well as the type. All leave behind them a glaucous-grey seed capsule or head which is most attractive. I think that the plants are worth growing for this alone. If these are gathered early enough, soon after the petals fall, they will keep their pleasant grey-green hue. When they are ripe these heads become a biscuit colour, both light and dark.

These capsules never grow as large as the imported ones, usually about an inch in diameter going right down to the merest fraction. Much depends, of course, on how long they are left on the plant. At the end of the season I pull up any plants and let them dry. From these I get a variety of heads

145

of all sizes which I use in swags, cones and arrangements of all kinds. The stems are hollow and they may easily be wired and mounted by passing a wire up through the stem.

For use in arrangements, imported heads usually need lengthening considerably. All sizes can be mounted and arranged in the form of a bunch of grapes, sometimes useful for the centre of a large arrangement. Cut the stems quite short or they will get in the way.

I find that the large imported heads are often damaged at the 'crown', that prettily shaped top to the capsule. To improve this, cut the remains away exposing a small hole in the top. Carefully cut away a good crown from a garden poppy and stick this on in the place of the other.

## Physalis

Sometimes the full stems of physalis are difficult to coax into the position where their bright lanterns will hang to the best advantage. It is possible to insert a wire up the stem for some inches so that the stem base can be bent or curved. Often more effective is to attach a false stem or a couple of strong mount wires. The physalis can then be angled as required before the false stem is inserted into the container.

Individual lanterns can be used in a variety of ways. You can, for example, wire several to one long stem thus making a super stem. They can be mounted individually and used in cones, swags and arrangements.

Lanterns can be cut open to reveal the berry and thus form 'flowers'. These can be mounted on stem wires and used as individuals. They can also be assembled into attractive sprays.

To make the 'flowers', cut the orange case into five or six petals, following as a guide the tiny pointed openings at its base. If the berry is pierced when the flowers are mounted it will show signs of bruising in these open flowers, so fasten the wire to the tiny stems instead of pushing it into the centre of the lantern.

## Walnuts and others

By using nuts in arrangements and other ensembles you can introduce new and interesting textures and forms. Stemmed nuts and their cases, acorns for instance, offer few problems so far as mounting is concerned but fallen chestnuts, both the sweet kind and conkers, do!

If the outer burrs of the former are to be used, these may be mounted by passing a wire right round their centres. It becomes quite inconspicuous.

I find that the best way of mounting the conkers is merely to push an 18g wire into the skin and flesh. Even after this treatment the nut will last for years. I use these in swags.

Walnuts can be mounted by piercing with a wire the soft portion which falls between the two valves, and pushing it in until it is firmly embedded. You can also mount them by taking a long, light-gauge wire and passing this round the nuts in such a way that it fits in the join made by the two halves. After doing this, hold the centre of the wire against the top of the nut while the two ends are twisted tightly round each other below the nut to form the 'stem'.

I save good half walnut shells to use in swags. These can be difficult to mount and the best way I have found is as follows. I use a fine, dark rose wire which is very thin. I take it round the middle of the shell lengthwise. Once again, it is held firmly at one end while the wires are twisted round each other below the other end.

The trick of drilling a hole through all tough skinned nuts and seeds, wooden fruits and cones, with a red hot implement is an old one but well worth knowing. If you have a drill and are handy with it so much the better for then quite large cones and any unfamiliar but woody seed capsule or fruit can be tackled.

Incidentally, one often comes upon some material which presents a problem. Always consider mounting it by passing a wire right round it. This is so often the best way and it is surprising how little the wire shows. Usually, the mounted material has to be quite closely scrutinised before it is evident. Another way I have found of mounting really heavy, though not necessarily large objects, is to use two single-legged mounts and to have one twisted one way and the other in the opposite direction.

Some of the seed capsules and cases sent to me from tropical trees are really very handsome but troublesome to mount and consequently to use. These often need a thick gauge wire.

# CHAPTER 11

# Arrangement

Once you have handled perpetuelles you will soon realise that they offer you many styles and forms of arrangement. One of the greatest things in their favour is that they are not likely to fade and for this reason can be arranged out of water. This factor alone opens up many possibilities! Not least of these is the fact that since no water is needed it is not essential to use a vessel to hold it and the flowers which stand in it. There are many ways and means of arranging dried flowers ex-container.

For a start, you can forget all about vases and think instead of displaying the flowers some other way, on the wall for instance, perhaps arranged on bark, a slice of wood, rush and cork mats, plaques, scrolls, banners, ribbons or simply inside a frame like any other picture.

## Making flower pictures

Each year I like to make one or more perpetuelle 'paintings' for my home or to give away to friends, and over the years I have come to like this way of displaying these special plant materials as well as any other. (See plate p125.)

## ARRANGEMENT

Making them can be as absorbing as painting a picture, and it is a picture which is three dimensional. Although the flowers are one's paints, colour is not all, for shapes, patterns and textures play their part.

Part of the interest in making the picture lies in finding both the frames and the materials. If I can buy a variety of old frames at some sale or junk shop, I find that my imagination is more often spurred by some lovely piece of craftsmanship than if I stand looking at a modern pseudo-wood frame. However, I hasten to add that even these are used from time to time. Fortunately, perpetuelles can be arranged to suit any setting, modern or period.

Whether or not you protect the flowers with glass really depends on how long you plan to keep the picture and, I suppose, how clean is the atmosphere in which it hangs. If glass is used it must not flatten the materials; it is necessary to separate from it the board on which they are mounted. This can be done by fixing a beading behind the frame. A great deal depends on the depth of the frame.

The flowers are then arranged on the board; the frame, with the glass attached in such a way that it is held and will not fall, is then fitted over them and the two portions joined together.

What kind of backing one uses on which to display the perpetuelles is really a matter of taste and personal choice. Obviously, it should harmonise both with the flowers and the frame and even the 'mood' of the arrangement. Hessian, even clean sacking, can be used for some designs. So can plain and coloured paper, silk, coarse linen, velvet, baize and many other materials. A plain rush mat makes a most pleasing foil and so does net of one colour stretched over another, both supporting harmonising colours.

Accomplished flower arrangers should find no difficulty in placing the flowers but the newcomer is recommended to

150

grade them, placing the largest daisy-like or 'faced' flowers, such as acrocliniums and pansies (pressed blooms are ideal in pictures), at the centre of the design, at its focal point, with the buds, ferns and leaves at the extremes. The flowers between should gradually taper in size from the large ones at the centre.

I like to make a bunch or sheaf of flowers rather than a haphazard scattering but, once again, this is a matter of personal choice. I have seen some very beautiful, interesting and contemporary 'montage' decorations where the accent was on textures rather than colour.

Technique is simple but this is a pursuit for the patient. Even a small picture can take hours if one pays proper attention to detail. Using a transparent adhesive, apply only the merest touch to all but thick daisies and others. Long stems, grasses, fern fronds, curving rhodanthe, seed heads such as saponaria, will need a dab at the stem base and on some part of the top. Even rounded seed heads such as poppies will need only a very little on the most rounded part of the capsule where it touches the mount.

I usually begin at the centre or focal point and gradually work to the edges. It is important when making 'bunches' to give the impression that the flowers really are bunched. This means that all parts should appear to flow from a central point, and although a stem on the very outer edges may appear to flow from the centre it is seldom necessary to take it all the way. If you did so, the arrangement would soon become too bulky and you would have to stick one piece of material to another. I try to fix each to the mount. Sometimes a piece might be half on the mount and half on a piece tucked under it. Examples of this are when I show a little fern frond arranged behind a flower or two or three tiny leaves surrounding a bloom. Stems such as grasses can really be kept quite short and some other item can be arranged in such a way that the base of the grass stem is hidden. If the base of each item that is not completely round, is pointed towards the centre, the result will be right.

I feel that it is important to give bunches and sheaves a stem portion which is an integral part of the design. This is arranged independently by which I mean that the stems shown seldom belong to any particular item in the top portion of the bunch. I use fine straws, and usually only the tops need adhesive. These are pushed up under the flower or flowers at the centre and those near the base of the bunch. Here also I like to use a few tapering materials flowing down on each side of the stems—but not too far down. Sometimes I let one or two flow from the centre of the bunch across the top of the stem portion. The ends of tiny fern fronds, even a piece of pressed moss, look well used this way. Buds, tiny leaves, delicate seed heads and tiny pressed flowers or even the starry centres left after the seed has gone from such flowers as michaelmas daisies, groundsel and other miniature 'daisies', individual awns from grasses, the cones from cupressus and thuja, are all materials I use so that the stalks flow naturally from a diminishing portion of the bunch and do not give the impression of having been stuck on.

Quite often these extra small items have to be arranged with tweezers. After placing any piece, give it a light press to make sure that it comes in contact with the mount. (See plate p126.)

Besides being arranged in bunches, sheaves and other patterns or designs the materials can simulate a flower arrangement in a container of some kind. Natural vessels are easily found, large poppy heads, walnuts, acorn cups and other 'vase'-shaped cups and capsules can be halved and used for this purpose. Flat sea shells make good containers and there are so many sizes in these.

Such containers are best applied to the mount after the flower materials have, in the main, been arranged. A few tiny blooms, leaves and seed heads may be allowed to flow over the rim of the container so that the two parts are not too obviously separated. It is best first to outline the container on the mount with pencil for guidance.

For unframed flower groups you can use a multitude of other mounts—there seems to be no limit, I've seen them even on plates!

In Scandinavia I saw ribbons hung like bell pulls at the side of a fireplace. The perpetuelles were arranged along the centre, lengthwise. The ribbon had a fringed base and a cord for hanging at the top. Along these two edges a 'beading' of tiny flowers had been arranged.

Those who want to try to turn this craft into a financial proposition may care to make calendars as well as plaques of all kinds. If these are well done there is always a market for them.

## Gift wraps

For years now my gift wraps at Christmas, and at certain other times too, have been made more fun and more distinctive by little decorations made from perpetuelles. These are arranged and assembled in various ways. On a round parcel, drum-like, or else topping a cylindrical package, I might place a little garland made from a variety of things, the brown berry-like seeds of hypericum, acorns, small cones, leaves and the smallest flowers. These harmonise with the paper round the gift and the ribbon which secures it. Elsewhere, the ribbon bow surrounds a 'corsage' type spray or bunch made perhaps of five shadow, skeletonised holly leaves, brown cones and a few red helichrysum or perhaps dyed gnaphalium in clusters, berry-like. Christmas

153

roses made from honesty are backed with preserved ivy and leather brown glossy camellia foliage. Sometimes one large cone is transformed into a miniature Christmas tree, the shape is very similar, and garlanded with tiny perpetuelles and stood on a flat package. All the ingredients for these decorations have first to be mounted on fine wires and I usually tape them so that there is no danger of wire ends scratching or tearing.

At this time also, I make many garlands and swags. Some are for wall and door decorations. Others will fit round the base of candlesticks to make low table decorations. All are made by the method explained in the previous chapter whether they are great or small.

'Wooden' swags in the style of a Grinling Gibbons carving, are used here and there in my home as frames for a mirror. Those that hang at the sides have a topknot of a fan of leaves rising from the back of the swag or rope. Quite often I use rhododendron, turned so that the rusty-tan felted underside, tomentum, is seen.

Elsewhere a single rope, some 2-3ft in length, 6in wide at the top, tapering to 1in, hangs on a wall near an old mahogany desk and alongside maplewood picture frames. The 'wood' with wood theme is both decorative and extremely pleasing. 'Furniture' of this kind is distinctive and very cheap!

But the chief flower arrangement features of this season are the Byzantine cones which I make from a great variety of perpetuelles, sometimes in a mixture, sometimes of one kind.

## Byzantine cones

Usually the cones are made in a container. Sometimes they are set on a flat base, a cake board for example. This depends on where they are to stand when they are finished.

I like them best in containers that have a foot for then the cone is 'lifted' attractively. (See plates p143.)

The foundation into which the materials are fixed can be wire-netting packed with damp moss (damp so that the wires will rust and hold), or any of the many good plastics ready-shaped cones now marketed everywhere. These vary from being very hard, in which case only really tough un-brittle stems can be inserted or only wired materials, to the soft Oasis and Oasis-type composition which will take the most fragile of stems yet stay intact. As you would expect, the latter is the easiest to work with but often you need the firm support, especially when heavy items such as pine cones are being used.

Wire-netting can be quite satisfactory and I recommend it where really large cones are to be made. It is best first to cut a strong paper pattern, then to lay this on the small-mesh netting. Incidentally, if you spray this with gold or silver paint before arranging the cone materials it will not be necessary to hide the entire surface. Any which shows through will not look unsightly.

To draw the cone on the paper in the first place, tie a thread to a pencil, making the thread the height of the tree. Pin the thread in one corner and describe an arc with the pencil point. Cut along the arc and curve the paper to decide how wide or slender the cone should be and then trim accordingly.

Chalk round the outline of the paper pattern and cut through the wire, following the mark with florist scissors. These are quicker and easier to use than wire clippers. They should be part of every flower arranger's kit.

A cone can be rested on the rim of a container in which case it is often possible to push the rim in the base a little way so that the cone is firmly held and will not tilt. Alternatively, it can be mounted on a stem. I use bamboos of varying thicknesses according to the size of the cone and I cover them with stem paper or some other tape. Its colour should harmonise with the materials in the finished article.

Any stem must be well anchored. It is possible to use more wire-mesh inside the container as a stem-holder or, in the case of light-weight designs, any foamed plastic made for this purpose. But I often use a quick-drying plaster such as Polyfilla to hold the stems, especially when the finished cone they are to support is likely to be heavy.

Rather than spoil the container for any likely further use by pouring the wet plaster directly in it, I first line it with cooking foil. When the time comes to empty it, the entire plaster block can be lifted out.

When firm plastic cones are used as foundations it helps to sharpen the point of the cane a little before pushing it inside the centre of the shape.

When materials of all one kind, poppy seed heads for instance, are to be used and where they vary in size, it is best to grade them before arrangement so that the very smallest can be set at the apex. When large or projecting items are to be used it is sometimes necessary first to cover the whole surface of the cone with some filler or fabric so that any spaces between them are ready fillled. Alternatively, this can be done as assembly progresses. It all depends on the type. For instance, a cone made entirely of helichrysums is not likely to need fillers except for decorative contrast should this be desired, whereas medium-sized pine cones, which taper to their tips, may need something alternated between them. Evergreens such as curly cupressus, limonium of the latifolium type, seed head clusters such as *Sedum spectabile* are examples. Insert the main materials in one ring or part of a ring to determine if a filler is necessary before beginning work.

Usually, cones are built up by making concentric rings

round them. I find it best to begin from the base and work to the tip simply because I have found that in this way successive insertions tend not to disturb those inserted earlier. Stems or mount wires should not be too long or one will disturb the other. On the other hand, if they are too short the materials will not become properly anchored and will fall out either as work proceeds or later.

I usually vary the angle at which I insert the stems and wires, pushing them slightly upwards to the apex in the lower portions, horizontal in the central zones and slightly downwards as I progress higher up the cone. The item at the apex has its stem or wire inserted vertically.

The under part of the cone, the base, should be covered if the cone is raised on a stem. You may like to finish off the base with a final frill of leaves or some contrasting material. This often looks best when the cone sits on the container but it is really a matter for the designer to decide for much depends on what materials are used in the main part of the cone.

Variations can be played on the cone theme and instead of slowly tapering the flowers or other materials, the outline can curve in the centre, like a pineapple. This design is often more amusing and effective if the top is accentuated by arranging a tuft of leaves or some other materials, grasses perhaps, in this position.

## Tree arrangements

As well as conical plastic shapes it is also possible to buy globes in several sizes. These can be mounted on stems, in exactly the same way as described for cones, to make little 'trees' which can look very decorative, especially as pairs, for sideboards and mantelpieces. Tall trees, a mass of foliage and flowers, look well on each side of an inner doorway.

## ARRANGEMENT

When planning to arrange any materials on a foundation, bear in mind that the finished design will be much wider and taller for it will consist of twice the length of the materials to be mounted plus the diameter of the cone, globe or whatever.

If you want to make a much larger design than you could by arranging the components sessile on the foundation, mount them on equal size wires, double-legged method or, if they are to be unwired, cut equal stems of the length you require.

I have found that the introduction of plastic stem-holders has made a tremendous difference in the ease with which perpetuelles can be arranged. I use Oasis almost exclusively nowadays but I use it in conjunction with other things at most times. The plastic itself is very light in weight and so, generally speaking, are most dried materials. To arrange them in Oasis alone would be like putting them in an empty container. Unless this was made of some very heavy substance there would be the danger of the arrangements becoming knocked over or disarranged in some way. This being so, I weight all containers with sand or gravel. The cylinder or block of Oasis is placed on this.

For those readers who haven't used these foamed urea plastics perhaps I should point out their advantages. Only a small portion of a stem needs to be inserted for it to be held firmly. This is a great advantage for so many of the materials we have to use have short stems. It means, for instance, that you can often arrange a leaf simply by pushing its short petiole in the surface of a block. (See plate p143.)

No less important is the fact that stems can be arranged at any angle, even upside down. This has proved tremendously useful and has helped me produce some unusual and pretty designs. For instance, I like to make mass arrangements of dainty blooms, usually statice, acroclinium and rhodanthe, in pedestal vases. If I place the block of Oasis so that it projects well above the rim of the container and sometimes even over its rim (this is done by pushing its rim into the plastic and not vice-versa) I can give my arrangements greater depth yet retain the flowers' daintiness. Instead of arranging the low stems at rim level and angling them in such a way that the blooms or leaves flow over it, I can actually arrange them by pointing their stems vertically into the plastic towards the tip of the design. This means that flowers often flow parallel to the pedestal itself. Rhodanthe, whose blooms are drooping and pendulous by nature, look enchanting arranged this way and I can usually angle statice and other flowers so that the full value of even the slightest curve is exploited. (See plate p144.)

When I am making large arrangements and also when I am likely to use heavy perpetuelles, which may either have thick stems or be mounted on wires, I use a combination of gravel, Oasis and wire-netting. The plastic is placed below the netting and not too far down inside the container, to take just the bases of any fine stems, such as long grasses and cereals for instance, and others which may be passed down through the netting. The netting mesh itself, which usually protrudes a little way above the rim, is capable of holding any stems firmly including those which may have to be passed through it almost horizontally. And sometimes materials that are spliced to false stems in order to get them to fall at a certain angle, have to be arranged like this.

Quite often I use wire-netting alone or, should the container not be heavy, wire-netting on gravel. This is when I know that the materials can be arranged easily this way and still keep their positions. These are usually branches of foliage, seed heads and others on their own thick stems.

Large wide-spreading branches are fairly simply arranged.

159

## ARRANGEMENT

A pin-holder should be placed on the floor of the container, held in place either with 'pills' or washers of plasticine or Oasisfix, and the branch ends impaled on this after they have been stripped.

If smaller branches are to be arranged at rim level, wire-netting can be placed on the holder and should fill the container to just above the rim. Stems to be arranged vertically can be pushed right down until they are impaled on the points while the smaller branches can be inserted through the netting at various angles.

A way to get a branch of foliage to flow prettily outwards or downwards is to cut it a certain way before arrangement. Choose a lateral stem, cut away the main stem above it and then cut it, not close to the main stem so that it is independent of it, but with a good portion still retained below it. So that it is, in effect, still at an angle to the main stem. For arrangement, insert the main stem portion only.

Wire-netting can be crumpled and used as a stem-holder for almost every purpose, especially the large-mesh type which is much more malleable than the small. Usually it is cut to fit the container. It should be a little over twice the width of the widest part and twice the depth. If, when the netting is cut and folded to place in position, the cut ends are placed uppermost they can be used as an aid in arrangement. They can be hooked over the rim of a container to anchor the rest of the netting, and can also be used to grip stems so that they are further supported.

When a very tall stem or some other very tall and perhaps heavy materials are to be arranged, it will help if twice the normal amount of wire-netting is cut and in this case it should project well above the rim of the container so long as it can be camouflaged later.

If the container is not precious then plaster can be used to hold a tall and heavy stem. It may be necessary to wedge this in position while the plaster is drying. Usually the simplest way to do this is to place two bricks or blocks of wood on the rim of the container close to the stem.

Where the container is wide enough in some part, an upturned flowerpot will hold a heavy branch in position quite firmly. Trim the stem end so that it can be pushed through the drainage hole of the pot until it holds firm and stays in place. If other things are to be arranged with the branch the area over the pot and round the stem can be filled with wire-netting and/or Oasis to take their stems.

As I explained earlier, a framework arrangement of perpetuelles can be enlivened by a focal point of fresh materials. In some cases, when fruit and vegetables are used for instance, these can be mounted and merely inserted in the correct position where they will last for some weeks. But when fresh berries, branches and even flowers are to be used, these will last better if they can reach water. For these, a separate container within the larger one should be provided.

Green conical metal vases can be bought from the florist and these are quite easy to thrust down into the wire-netting or whatever other stemholder might be used. Other small vessels such as tablet tubes and cigar tubes will do quite well for small arrangements. If these are put in place empty while the rest of the arrangement takes place the stems of the perpetuelles will not be disturbed or damaged at some later date.

If it is wished to place fresh materials, or indeed any kind, at higher levels in an arrangement than their stems will reach naturally, the cone or tube can be fastened to a cane by adhesive tape or, if it is to reach a considerable height, by two canes, one on each side of the supplementary container.

Heavy or much curving branches, such as driftwood, can

be difficult to arrange so that they will remain in place no matter how much the arrangement is moved around. Much depends on how they are to be used. For instance, if the piece is to stand on a low flat base consisting of a slice of wood, it is usually possible merely to screw one to the other.

Where the wood has to stand in a taller container it might be possible to fix it in wire-netting just like any other stem. I have often both spliced and wire-mounted driftwood and branches to make this easier. The false stem goes right down through the stem holder and makes a good anchor.

Sometimes it is best to screw a foot on the base of the wood, and in this case a cross-piece which will fit snugly at the base of the container and there hold firm, is to be recommended.

At other times, branches can be held by a kubari-type support. This is a Y-shaped piece of wood, usually cleft and hard cypress is good for this purpose, wedged across the container just below the rim where it is out of sight. This is the method often employed for arrangement of solitary branches but should you wish to arrange other materials, wire-netting and other stemholders can be placed over the kubari at a point where they would not disturb the arrangement of the branch.

Driftwood reminds me of shells and other marine accessories used by flower arrangers. Shells seem to have an affinity with perpetuelles which isn't so surprising when one remembers that many of the latter are merely shells of another kind. They can be used in arrangements as well as serve as containers for the plant materials. I find the latter quite charming, especially for some of the softly coloured flowers.

When very narrow-necked containers are to be used, such as stone bottles, wicker-covered wine jars or slim-waisted ceramic vases, it may be most helpful to arrange most of the materials in the hand before inserting them. This way the stem portion can be kept slim. The lowest ingredients can be mounted individually on wires which should then be bound, not twisted round, to the main stem. This should then be inserted but before doing this, measure it against the outside of the container to ensure that the main stem reaches to the base so that it will be properly supported.

Because they have been wire-mounted it should be possible, once the main stem is inserted, simply to pull the lowest items into their most attractive positions so that no sign of either wire or the neck of the container can be seen.

Try at all times to provide contrasts of shape. When you have many rounded shapes to arrange together, even if they are not of the same kind, look for some spicate form to go with them. Even a few grasses with helichrysum will look better than the straw daisies alone.

Grooming is important too! When you select a branch of preserved or pressed foliage, inspect it carefully and cut away all damaged leaves. Make sure that everything you use looks its best. Dried and faded are not terms synonymous with shabby! It is surprising how much fresher an arrangement can appear with everything in good condition, than one in which insect-eaten foliage, seed-fluffy everlastings and withered unstripped stem leaves, feature too prominently.

As I said earlier, the choice of containers is extremely important. Many flower arrangers tend to link age with age, searching out antique and old-fashioned vessels and containers for dried flower arrangements. This is sometimes a mistake. Much depends upon the setting I know, but modern containers often suit perpetuelles best, and they certainly seem to impart some of their freshness and modernity to them in the same way as some of the antique containers can suggest that the materials they hold are old. Its just a point, but worth watching.

Perpetuelles do look well in wood and wicker, but it must be clean, bright or polished. Any old basket, grimed with age, will simply cloud them with an overall greyness. Wicker can be scrubbed and painted, and white or a pale primrose-yellow paint will give a brighter and smarter effect than will gilt, silver, orange and red.

Polished wood containers, old ones this time, such as mahogany tea-chests and cutlery boxes or old workboxes are most attractive when filled with the right materials but avoid using grey and light-absorbing items for them. Use 'wooden' mixtures and cheerful light-reflecting straw daisies in warm hues.

Plain modern, beautifully turned bowls, canisters which originally were made for some other purpose, even boxes, all look right for some materials and some settings. In spite of it being sometimes difficult to polish them once they are filled, I like to use all kinds of metal vases as containers for every kind of perpetuelle, and you can easily find colour groupings suitable for brass, copper, silver, pewter and modern steel.

This book was to be mainly about dried flowers and plant materials themselves and not too much about their actual arrangement. On this subject I have written at greater length in some of my other books.

However, arranging perpetuelles does call forth other skills. It is not difficult to bring a liveliness to an arrangement of fresh flowers for so much of the job has already been done for us and a lovely flower is a lovely flower. But the savouring, as it were, of these perpetuelles really does whet the floral appetite. I am certain that the study of the structure of plant materials, the blending of unfamiliar textures and of harsh as well as soft colours, brings a greater understanding not only of their growth and of their arrangement when fresh but also of something of their nature. I hope that I have helped to further that understanding.

# Index

References to plate pages are printed in *italic*

# INDEX

# INDEX